DOCTOR WHO CLASSICS

VOLUME 2

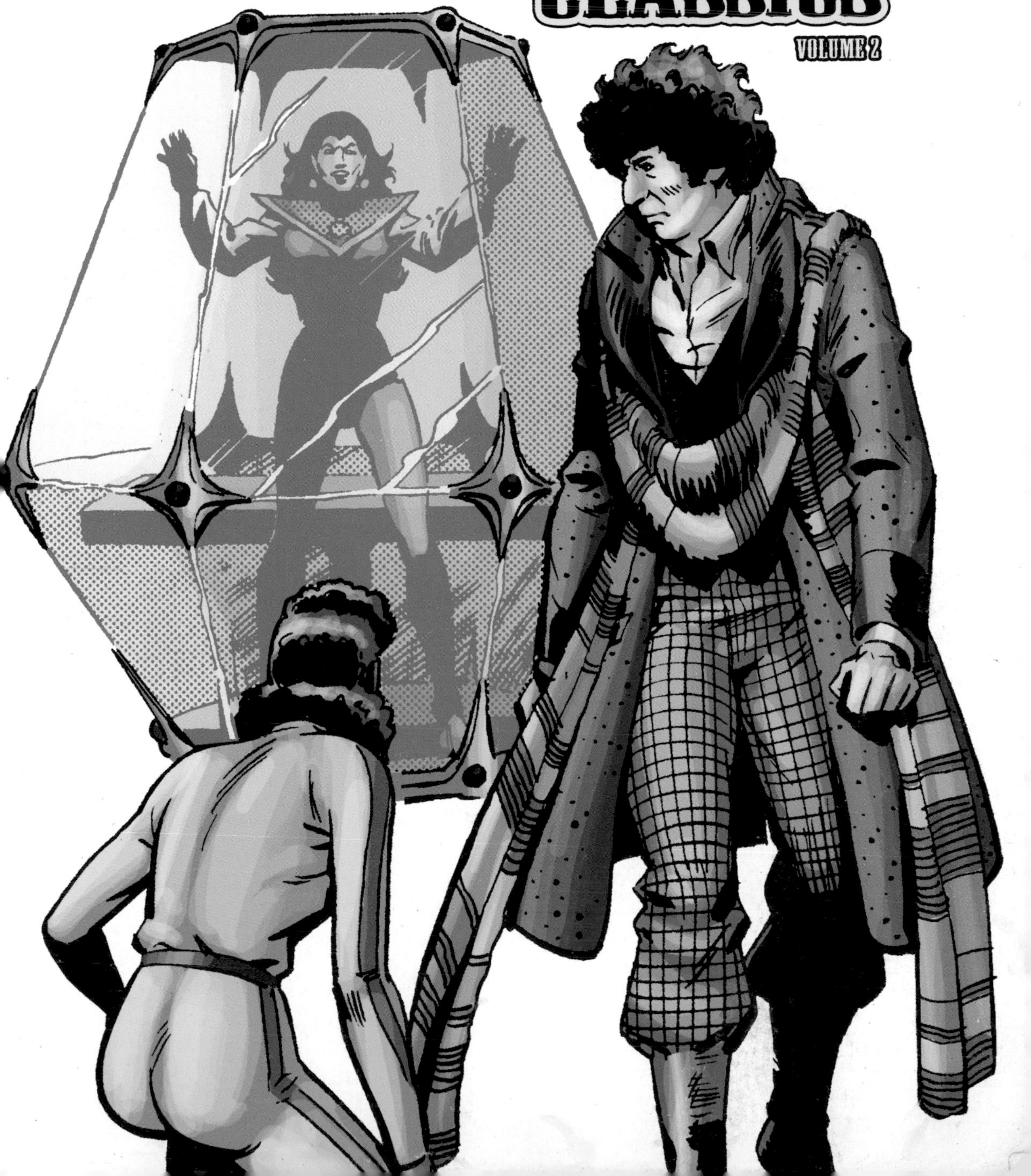

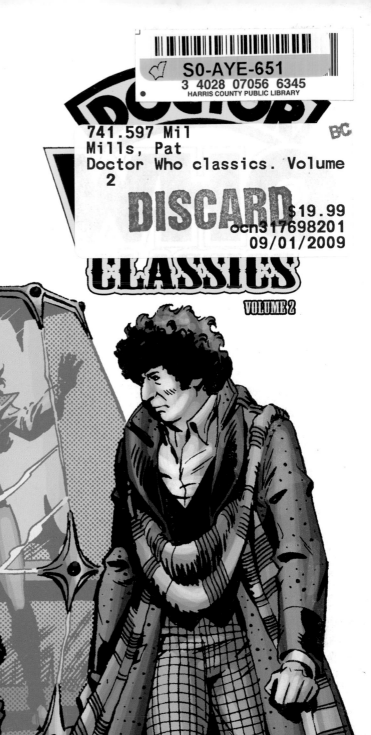

DOCTOR WHO CLASSICS VOLUME 2

Written by
Pat Mills & John Wagner
(pages 3–40)
and Steve Moore
(pages 41–115)

Art by
Dave Gibbons

Original Edits by
Dez Skinn and Paul Neary

Colors: Charlie Kirchoff
Cover: Charlie Kirchoff over Dave Gibbons
Series Edits: Chris Ryall
Collection Edits: Justin Eisinger
Collection Design: Chris Mowry

IDW Publishing
Operations:
Moshe Berger, Chairman
Ted Adams, Chief Executive Officer
Greg Goldstein, Chief Operating Officer
Matthew Ruzicka, CPA, Chief Financial Officer
Alan Payne, VP of Sales
Lorelei Bunjes, Dir. of Digital Services
Marci Hubbard, Executive Assistant
Alonzo Simon, Shipping Manager

Editorial:
Chris Ryall, Publisher/Editor-in-Chief
Scott Dunbier, Editor, Special Projects
Andy Schmidt, Senior Editor
Justin Eisinger, Editor
Kris Oprisko, Editor/Foreign Lic.
Denton J. Tipton, Editor
Tom Waltz, Editor
Mariah Huehner, Assistant Editor

Design:
Robbie Robbins, EVP/Sr. Graphic Artist
Ben Templesmith, Artist/Designer
Neil Uyetake, Art Director
Chris Mowry, Graphic Artist
Amauri Osorio, Graphic Artist

ISBN: 978-1-60010-289-9

11 10 09 08   1 2 3 4

Special thanks to Jordana Chapman and Anna Hewitt at BBC Worldwide, Dave Gibbons, Marc Mostman, and Mike Riddell and Tom Spilsbury at Panini Publishing, Ltd., for their invaluable assistance.

WWW.IDWPUBLISHING.COM

DOCTOR WHO
AND THE STAR BEAST

Stan Lee presents

THE MEEP — A GALACTIC SUPER-CRIMINAL — USES HIS SHIP'S STAR DRIVE TO ESCAPE FROM EARTH. AS A RESULT, BLACK CASTLE IS SUCKED INTO A BLACK HOLE WITH THE DOCTOR AT THE EPI-CENTRE!

FOR A MOMENT, THAT IS AN *INFINITY*, HE PLUNGES INTO A *NETHER-REALM*...WHERE ALL LIGHT IS *TRAPPED*...WHERE *TIME* AND *SPACE* DO NOT EXIST...

EXPERIENCING *PAIN BEYOND* ITS HUMAN MEANING!

AND THEN, MIRACULOUSLY, THE AWESOME POWER ABATES...MATTER STABILISES AGAIN...

GET THE DOCTOR DOWN!

BUT, UNDER THE TITANIC PRESSURES, FURNACES ERUPT, IRON WORK COLLAPSES AND METAL RUNS LIKE WAX...

TAKE MY TENTACLE!

WHAT HAPPENED, DOCTOR?

I REDUCED THE POWER OF THE MEEP'S STAR DRIVE...GIVING HIM JUST ENOUGH POWER TO LEAVE EARTH...

...CAUSING A TEMPORARY *TREMOR* IN HYPER-SPACE, RATHER THAN A *CATACLYSM*!

BUT ENOUGH TO DESTROY THESE STEEL MILLS! WE'VE *GOT* TO GET EVERYONE OUT ...*THE TARDIS*!

As the **radiation** wears off the **bewildered workers**, an **evacuation** begins...

We can't **all** fit in a **police box**!

Plenty of room inside! But not the second door on the left -- that's my bedroom!

PURRR!

K-9

Hello, K-9 -- I must get round to repairing you, old chap!

..Excuse me -- if I can just get to my **controls**!..

Meanwhile, the **Meep** is unaware of how the Doctor has **outwitted** him...

Soon the 'Most-High' will lead new armies! Again the Wrarth Galaxy will run with **blood**!

For I am the **saviour** of my race! I will save them from the **senility** of **peace**! The **decay** of **happiness**!

What's wrong with being **happy**?

Happiness is a stagnant pond! True joy can only be found through inflicting pain, Earth girl!

NO!

Suddenly!

Now hear this! You are under arrest! Any resistance and we blow you out of the cosmos!

MEEP! MEEP!

4

THE MEEP'S CRAFT IS SECURED -- A *BOARDING TUBE* SNAKES OUT...

THE *WRARTH WARRIORS!* B-BUT I SHOULD BE ON THE OTHER SIDE OF THE UNIVERSE!

AS THE AIRLOCK DOOR IS CUT THROUGH...

THEY WON'T TAKE ME ALIVE! I'LL--

NO, YOU DON'T!

DON'T MOVE, CRIMINAL!

CHECK HIS *POUCH* FOR HIDDEN WEAPONS--THEN WE'LL GET THE *CUFFS* ON!

SOON AFTER, THE *TARDIS* MATERIALISES ...AND THE DOCTOR-- HAVING DELIVERED THE WORKERS TO SAFETY-- ALIGHTS...

DOCTOR!

I DO BELIEVE THIS IS WHERE WE CAME IN, K-9!

WHAT WILL HAPPEN TO THE MEEP, ZOGROTH?

HE WILL BE GIVEN A FAIR TRIAL, ACCORDING TO THE LAWS OF WRARTH! WE WILL ASK FOR ...*THE SUPREME PENALTY!*

HISSS!

PLEASE SHARON--I DON'T WANT TO DIE! I KNOW I'VE BEEN A BAD MEEP --BUT I'LL BE GOOD IN FUTURE!

TEARS RUN DOWN THE ALIEN'S CHEEKS...

IT-IT WASN'T MY FAULT ...I-I HAD AN *UNHAPPY CHILDHOOD*...OTHER MEEPS WERE A *BAD INFLUENCE* ON ME!

DON'T LET THEM CUT MY *FURRY LITTLE HEAD* OFF, SHARON!

BUT SHARON ISN'T FOOLED TWICE --

I *HATE* YOU! YOU'RE *HORRIBLE!*

MEEP! MEEP!

THE ALIEN IS LED AWAY TO A MAXIMUM SECURITY CELL...

THERE'S BEEN A *MISTAKE,* SIR. IT-IT'S MY *TWIN BROTHER* YOU WANT! *YOU'VE GOT THE WRONG MEEP!*

LET THE *JUSTICE OF WRARTH* BE DONE!

LATER...THE WARRIORS' BOMB IS REMOVED FROM THE DOCTOR AND HE PREPARES TO RETURN SHARON TO EARTH...

WE ARE IN YOUR DEBT, DOCTOR. PERHAPS WE WILL MEET AGAIN! I CAN RECOMMEND MY PLANET FOR A *HOLIDAY...*

...THE *SULPHURIC ACID SEAS* ARE DELIGHTFUL -- AND THE *SMELL* FROM THE *METHANE BOGS...* MMM! IT'S... GOOD!

MAYBE I'LL TRY IT INSTEAD OF *BENIDORM!*

AS SHARON ENTERS THE *TARDIS* ...

BLIMEY! IT'S ... *INCREDIBLE!* YOU'RE REALLY *DIFFERENT,* DOCTOR...MOST PEOPLE HAVE BOSSES AN' BILLS AN' NOSEY NEXT DOOR NEIGHBOURS...

...BUT I COULDN'T IMAGINE *YOU* WITH A *MORTGAGE!*

WHAT AN *AWFUL THOUGHT!* I'D RATHER FACE *THE BLACK GUARDIAN* HIMSELF!

HISSS!

THE END.

NEXT ISSUE JOIN THE DOCTOR, SHARON AND K-9 IN... **DEVIL-SPAWN!**

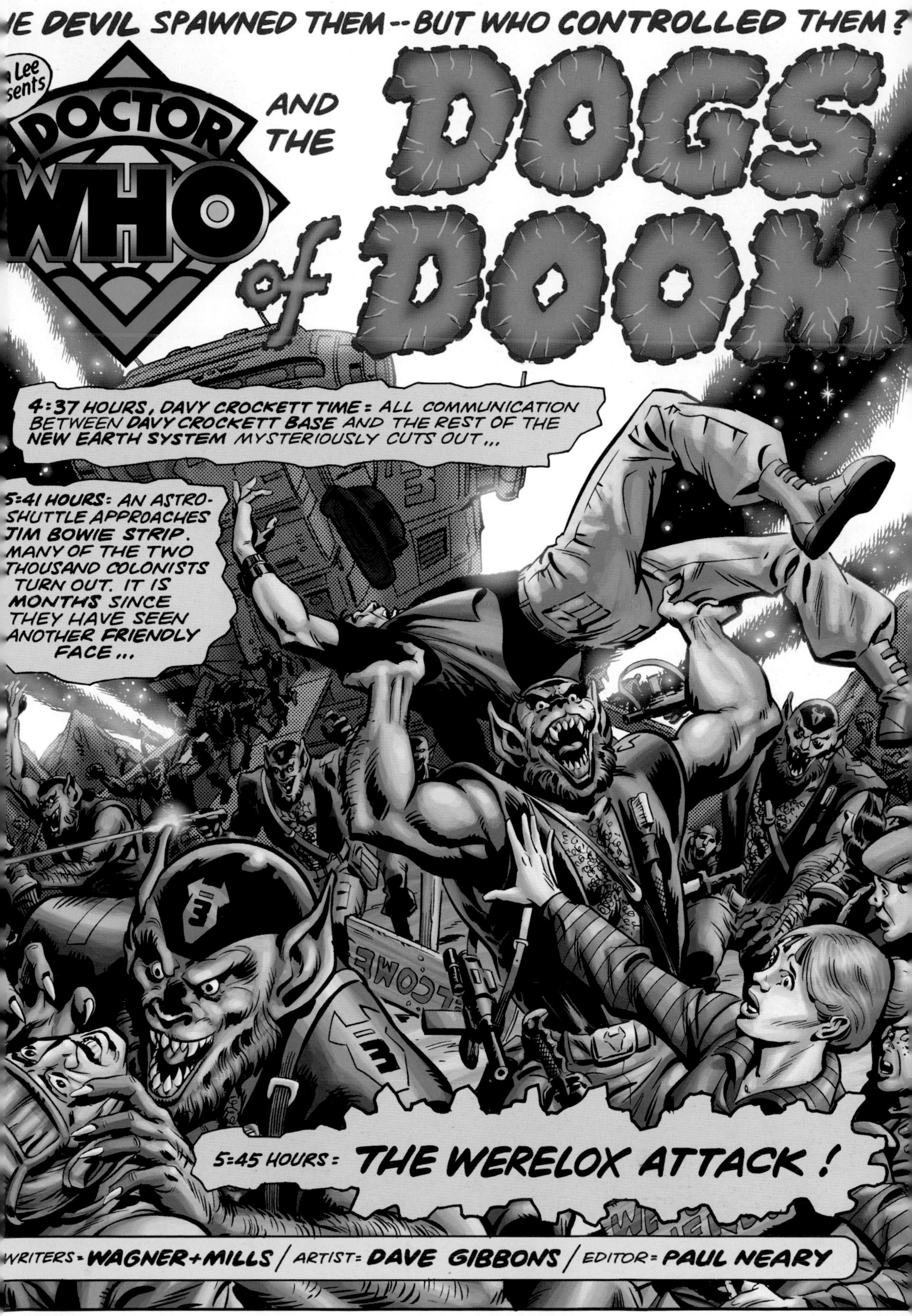

IE DEVIL SPAWNED THEM--BUT WHO CONTROLLED THEM?
Lee sents
DOCTOR WHO
AND THE
DOGS of DOOM
4:37 HOURS, DAVY CROCKETT TIME: ALL COMMUNICATION BETWEEN DAVY CROCKETT BASE AND THE REST OF THE NEW EARTH SYSTEM MYSTERIOUSLY CUTS OUT...
5:41 HOURS: AN ASTRO-SHUTTLE APPROACHES JIM BOWIE STRIP. MANY OF THE TWO THOUSAND COLONISTS TURN OUT. IT IS MONTHS SINCE THEY HAVE SEEN ANOTHER FRIENDLY FACE...
5:45 HOURS: THE WERELOX ATTACK!
WRITERS= WAGNER+MILLS / ARTIST= DAVE GIBBONS / EDITOR= PAUL NEARY

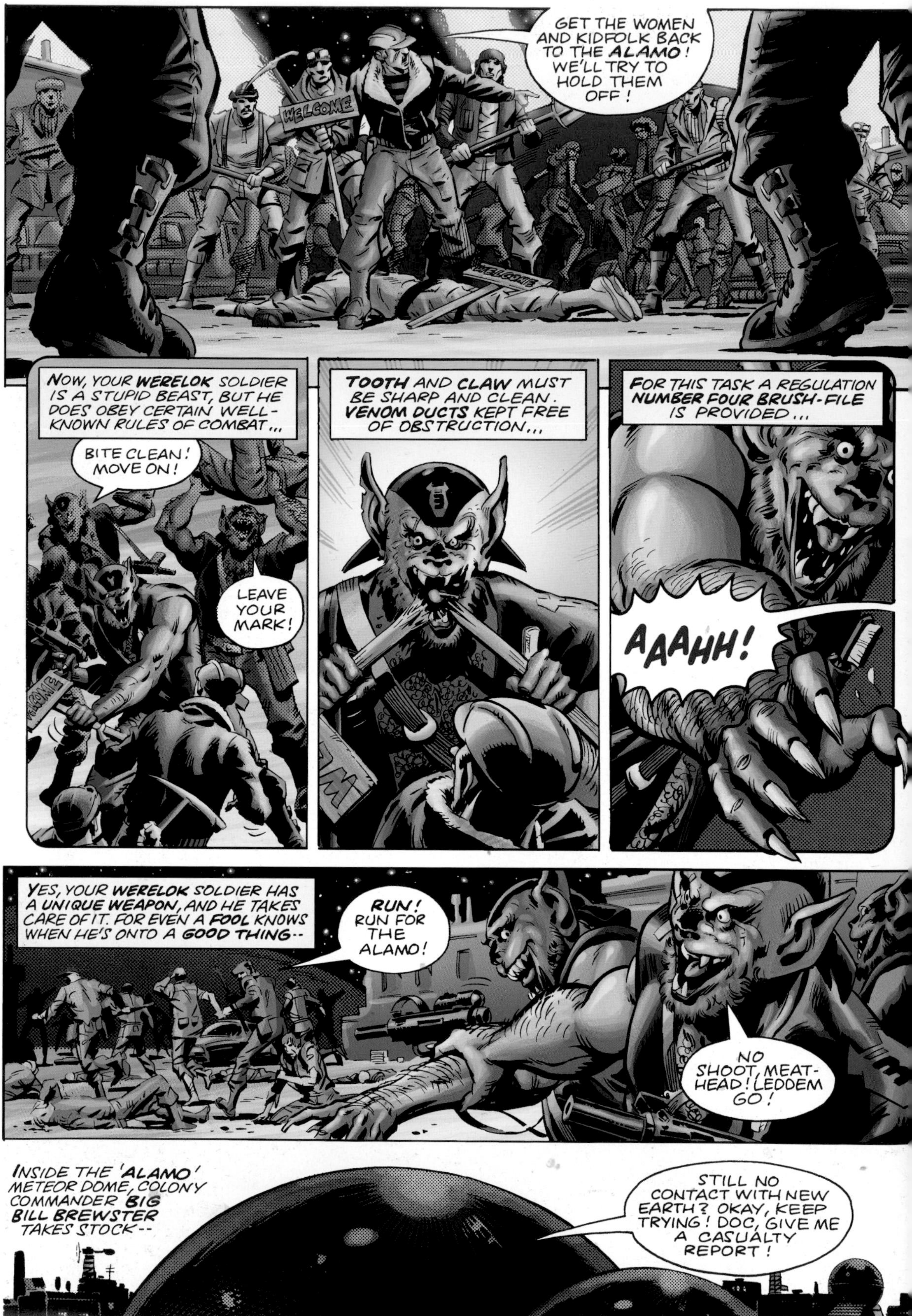

GET THE WOMEN AND KIDFOLK BACK TO THE ALAMO! WE'LL TRY TO HOLD THEM OFF!
WELCOME
NOW, YOUR WERELOK SOLDIER IS A STUPID BEAST, BUT HE DOES OBEY CERTAIN WELL-KNOWN RULES OF COMBAT...
BITE CLEAN! MOVE ON!
LEAVE YOUR MARK!
TOOTH AND CLAW MUST BE SHARP AND CLEAN. VENOM DUCTS KEPT FREE OF OBSTRUCTION...
FOR THIS TASK A REGULATION NUMBER FOUR BRUSH-FILE IS PROVIDED...
AAAHH!
YES, YOUR WERELOK SOLDIER HAS A UNIQUE WEAPON, AND HE TAKES CARE OF IT. FOR EVEN A FOOL KNOWS WHEN HE'S ONTO A GOOD THING--
RUN! RUN FOR THE ALAMO!
NO SHOOT, MEAT-HEAD! LEDDEM GO!
INSIDE THE 'ALAMO' METEOR DOME, COLONY COMMANDER BIG BILL BREWSTER TAKES STOCK--
STILL NO CONTACT WITH NEW EARTH? OKAY, KEEP TRYING! DOC, GIVE ME A CASUALTY REPORT!

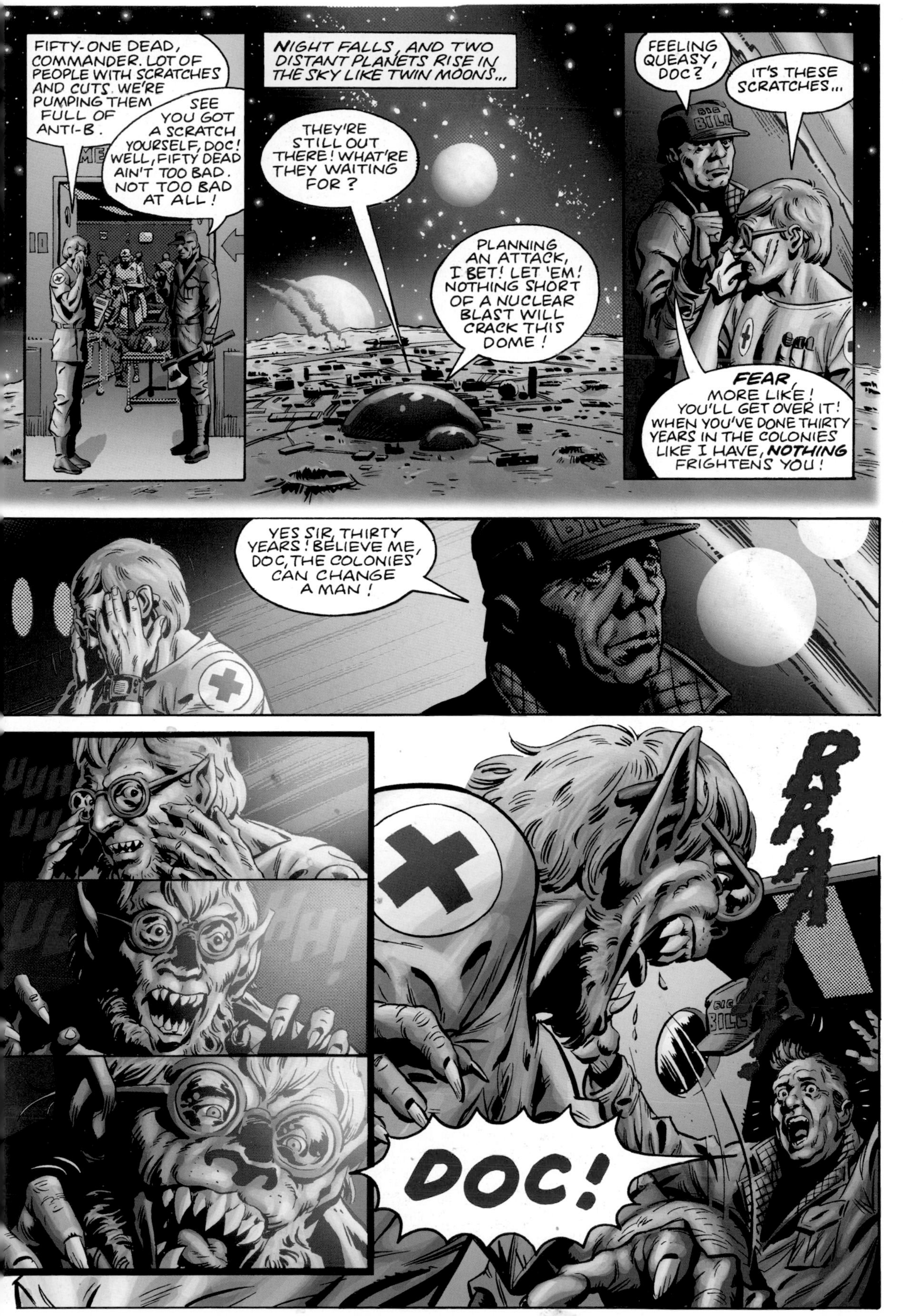
FIFTY-ONE DEAD, COMMANDER. LOT OF PEOPLE WITH SCRATCHES AND CUTS. WE'RE PUMPING THEM FULL OF ANTI-B.
SEE YOU GOT A SCRATCH YOURSELF, DOC! WELL, FIFTY DEAD AIN'T TOO BAD. NOT TOO BAD AT ALL!
NIGHT FALLS, AND TWO DISTANT PLANETS RISE IN THE SKY LIKE TWIN MOONS...
THEY'RE STILL OUT THERE! WHAT'RE THEY WAITING FOR?
PLANNING AN ATTACK, I BET! LET 'EM! NOTHING SHORT OF A NUCLEAR BLAST WILL CRACK THIS DOME!
FEELING QUEASY, DOC?
IT'S THESE SCRATCHES...
FEAR, MORE LIKE! YOU'LL GET OVER IT! WHEN YOU'VE DONE THIRTY YEARS IN THE COLONIES LIKE I HAVE, NOTHING FRIGHTENS YOU!
YES SIR, THIRTY YEARS! BELIEVE ME, DOC, THE COLONIES CAN CHANGE A MAN!
DOC!

OH, MY GRIEF! ALL OF THEM!

BY 8:12 DAVY CROCKETT TIME, ALL HUMAN LIFE IS EXTINGUISHED...

NEW EARTH CONTROL, THIS IS JOE BEAN IN TANGO ONE TWO COMIN' IN ATCHA PAST THE COONSKIN PLANET--

I'M COOKIN' ONE FIVE HOTDOGS HERE, TWO WITH MUSTARD! REQUESTIN' CLEARANCE FOR BIG MAMA, COME BACK--

BLAST, CAN'T PICK 'EM UP! SOMETHING'S JAMMIN' THE SQUAWK BOX!

MERCY SAKES!

BABE! GET UP HERE! YOU AIN'T GONNA BELIEVE THIS--

I DON'T BELIEVE IT, AN' I'M LOOKIN' AT IT!

HERE WE ARE, SHARON--BLACKCASTLE ENGLAND! WELL, PROBABLY BLACKCASTLE. YOU NEVER CAN BE SURE WITH THE TARDIS...

I CAN'T GET THE DOOR OPEN!

DEAR ME, YES! BREAKDOWN IN THE VERTICAL HOLD! IT'S HIGH TIME THE TARDIS HAD ITS TEN THOUSAND YEAR SERVICE...

THE DOCTOR CORRECTS THE FAULT--

BLACKCASTLE, ENGLAND, EARTH..?

AN' TIC TAC TOE TO YOU, GOOD BUDDY! HAUL YOUR JERKY OUT HERE AN' LET ME AN' BABE GET A LOOK ATCHA--

I'M THE DOCTOR. THIS IS SHARON AND K-9. I'M TRYING TO GET SHARON BACK TO EARTH. I APPEAR TO BE SLIGHTLY OFF TARGET...

LIGHT YEARS OFF, BUB! YOU'RE ON THE OTHER SIDE OF THE GALAXY!

THIS IS THE NEW EARTH SYSTEM! YOU'RE ON THE SPACEHOG, PRIDE AND JOY OF THE JOE BEAN HAULAGE LINE, INWARD BOUND FROM GAMMA ONE--

THE SPACEHOG

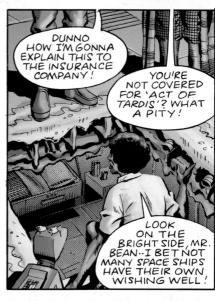

DUNNO HOW I'M GONNA EXPLAIN THIS TO THE INSURANCE COMPANY!

YOU'RE NOT COVERED FOR 'ACT OF TARDIS'? WHAT A PITY!

LOOK ON THE BRIGHT SIDE, MR. BEAN--I BET NOT MANY SPACE SHIPS HAVE THEIR OWN WISHING WELL!

SPARE ME THE SMART-SMARTS, BUDDY! GET YOUR FUNNY HUTCH OUTTA HERE! IT'S JAMMING MY RAYDIDDIO!

REALLY? IT'S MOST UNUSUAL FOR THE TARDIS TO INTERFERE WITH SIGNAL TRANSMISSION...

WHAAA--?

THAT MIGHT EXPLAIN THE PROBLEM!

NEXT WEEK: STRIKE HARD! STRIKE DEEP!

DOCTOR WHO
and the DOGS of DOOM

IN THE DISTANT NEW-EARTH SYSTEM, THE ASTRO-FREIGHTER 'SPACEHOG' COMES UNDER ATTACK FROM AN UNIDENTIFIED ENEMY BATTLECRAFT ...

TRACTOR BEAM! THEY'RE STOPPING US *DEAD!*

ABOARD THE BATTLECRAFT, WERELOK ASSAULT TROOPS PREPARE. PACK LEADER BRILL'S INSTRUCTIONS ARE REFRESHINGLY SIMPLE ...

KILL!

BRILL'S VICIOUSNESS ABOVE AND BEYOND THE CALL OF DUTY HAS WON HIS PACK THE TITLE OF 'THE FESTERING FORTY-NINTH'--

STRIKE HARD! STRIKE DEEP! NO WASTE TIME WID NEAT CLAW PATTERNS! DIS *WIPEOUT* RAID!

THEY'RE LAUNCHING LIMPET PODS!

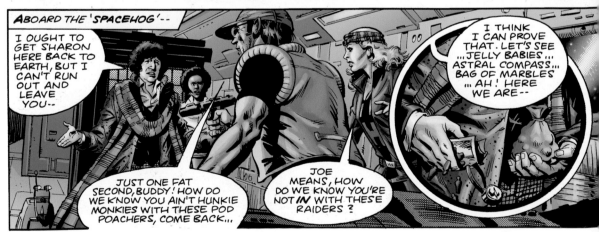

ABOARD THE 'SPACEHOG'--

I OUGHT TO GET SHARON HERE BACK TO EARTH, BUT I CAN'T RUN OUT AND LEAVE YOU--

I THINK I CAN PROVE THAT. LET'S SEE ...JELLY BABIES... ASTRAL COMPASS... BAG OF MARBLES ...AH! HERE WE ARE--

JUST ONE FAT SECOND, BUDDY! HOW DO WE KNOW YOU AIN'T HUNKIE MONKIES WITH THESE POD POACHERS, COME BACK...

JOE MEANS, HOW DO WE KNOW YOU'RE NOT *IN* WITH THESE RAIDERS?

A PHOTO OF ME ON THE BEACH ON THE PLANET VORLAG. THAT'S GOOM, THE PRIME VLAG -- TERRIBLY NICE CHAP -- AND AS *EVERYBODY KNOWS*, VLAGGANS WON'T BE SEEN *DEAD* WITH ANY- ONE OF *BAD CHARACTER*.

THAT'S GOOD ENOUGH FOR ME, JOE. THIS GUY'S TOO CRAZY TO BE DANGER- OUS!

STRAIGHT FOR THE COOKIE COOP, BABE! OKAY, GOOD BUDDY -- YOU'RE IN!

SHARON AND THE WOMAN RUN TO THE ENGINE DECK --

BABE ROTH'S MY NAME -- CO-OWNER AND ENGINEER OF THE *SPACEHOG*. THE ENGINE DECK'S THE SAFEST PLACE -- IF ANYPLACE IS SAFE!

AW, I'M NOT WORRIED! I'M GETTING USED TO FIGHTING CREATURES FROM SPACE!

I'M GONNA RIP HIS HOOK, BABE! SHOOT ME THAT MOOSE JUICE!

YOU GOT IT, JOE!

THE 'SPACEHOG'S' ENGINES FLARE --

WE'RE BEING BOARDED! YOUR CARGO, MAN -- IT'S CREATING TOO MUCH DRAG! *RELEASE IT!*

479

The SPACEHOG

THAT'S A BIG NIX, GOOD BUDDY! NO SELF-RESPECTIN' SPACE TRUCKER DITCHES HIS DOGS! THE *HOG* CAN DO IT, I TELL YA!

I HATE TO BE A BACK-SEAT DRIVER, BUT THERE'S REALLY NO TIME TO ARGUE!

THEY'RE BURNING THROUGH!

ITS BURDEN RELEASED, THE 'SPACEHOG' *RIPS* FREE--

NO BEAM CAN FOLLOW SUCH *HUGE ACCELERATION*--

INSIDE, AS JOE BEAN STRUGGLES TO REGAIN CONTROL--

THEY'RE IN!

SOME KIND OF *WOLVINE* RACE! K-9 -- DO YOUR STUFF!

YES, MASTER.

THE DOCTOR HAD REPAIRED K-9 --

STUN BEAM FUNCTIONING PERFECTLY, MASTER.

THANK GOODNESS FOR SMALL MERCIES! JOE! MORE BEHIND YOU!

'PRECIATE IT, GOOD BUDDY! CONSIDER 'EM JOE BEANED!

AAAAH!

K-9!

YOU! CHECKSEE OTHER PLACES!

YES, BRILL!

BRILL HANDLE DIS ONE!

NEXT WEEK: DEATH-MOON!

DOCTOR WHO
and the DOGS of DOOM

IN THE DISTANT NEW EARTH SYSTEM, THE ASTRO-FREIGHTER 'SPACE-HOG' IS UNDER ATTACK BY WERELOK SOLDIERS —

DOWN, BRILL! BE A GOOD DOG! MUSTN'T ATTACK THE DOCTOR!

YOU MAKE LAUGH AT BRILL! OTHERS LAUGH-- *ALL DIE!*

SCRIPT. MILLS & WAGNER ART. DAVE GIBBONS

BRILL'S CLAWS NO *FUNNY!*

AAAH!

BRILL KILL!

REGRET I CANNOT HELP YOU, MASTER.

NEVER MIND, K-9, I'LL THINK OF SOMETHING!

DON'T YOU KNOW IT'S *UNLUCKY* TO ATTACK *CRAZY* PEOPLE? AND *I'M* CRAZY--

SEE --I'VE LOST MY MARBLES!

HHRRRAA!

LET'S GET YOU BACK ON YOUR TREADS, K-9!

THE CREATURE IS STUNNED, MASTER.

TWO OF THEM WENT DOWN TO THE ENGINE DECK! SHARON AND BABE ARE THERE! COME ON, K-9!

STAND BY, MRS ROTH. I HAVE A PERSON TO PERSON *VIDEO* FROM MR BENSON IN LUTINE BELL, NEW EARTH...

THE COMMUNICATIONS MUST BE BACK ON!

IT'S *YOUNG FILBERT*, AGAIN, MRS ROTH! HE *DEACTIVATED* ME WHILE I WAS COOKING DINNER, THEN HE PAINTED MY HEAD-PARTS IN A MOST VILE AND DISGUSTING MANNER!

GRIEF! IT'LL HAVE TO WAIT, BENSON! I'M *BUSY*!

WHAT ARE THEY--?

I DUNNO, SHARON, BUT THEY'RE NOT FRIENDLY! *DOWN*!

THIS MATTER *WON'T* WAIT, MADAM! I MAY ONLY BE A *SERVO-ROBOT*, BUT I DO HAVE MY *DIGNITY*!

FOR HEAVEN'S SAKE, WHAT DO YOU WANT *ME* TO DO ABOUT IT?

YOU ARE THE BOY'S MOTHER, MADAM. YOU MUST SPEAK TO HIM. I HAVE HIM HERE--

HI, MA! I SHOWED STUFFY OLD BENSON, HUH! WHAT A LAUGH!

SEE WHAT I MEAN, MADAM!

I JUST HAVEN'T GOT TIME FOR THIS! **FILBERT!** YOU STOP MISTREATING BENSON OR I'LL PUNCH YOUR SNOOT WHEN I GET HOME! NOW **GOODBYE!**

I SEE WE'RE NOT NEEDED HERE!

BABE FIXED THEM, DOCTOR! SHE'S A REAL **SUPER-MUM!**

ON THE FLIGHT DECK, JOE BEAN IS RECOVERING --

LUCKY THEM LAZ-BURPS ONLY GREASED MY GURNEY OR I'D BE **TRUCKIN' HOTSIDE!** BETTER GET ON THE SQUAWK BOX TO BIG MAMA, FILL 'EM IN ON THE BEAN SCENE --

THE THREE SURVIVING WERELOX ARE TAKEN TO THE SMALL MED-BAY...

THIS WILL KEEP THEM QUIET WHEN K-9'S STUN BOLT WEARS OFF...

THEY REMIND ME OF WERE-WOLVES FROM ALL THOSE OLD HORROR MOVIES. WONDER IF THEY'RE WEARING MASKS --

THEY'RE REAL ENOUGH! I'VE GOT THE SCRATCHES TO PROVE IT! NOW IF YOU'LL LEAVE ME IN PEACE, I MAY BE ABLE TO DISCOVER MORE ABOUT THEM!

I EXPECT YOU'D LIKE TO CHANGE INTO SOMETHING MORE COMFORTABLE, SHARON. MY DAUGHTER LEFT SOME CLOTHES ON BOARD -- THEY SHOULD FIT YOU.

WISH I COULD GET AN EXCITING JOB LIKE YOURS, BABE!

I DIDN'T HAVE MUCH CHOICE. MY HUSBAND BEN WAS THE ENGINEER, BUT HE GOT KILLED -- FREAK ACCIDENT. I WAS LEFT WITH TWO KIDFOLK TO BRING UP AND HALF THE **SPACEHOG**...

IN BABE'S QUARTERS --

I'VE NEVER BEEN ON ANOTHER PLANET. WHAT'S **NEW EARTH** LIKE?

A LOT SMALLER THAN **YOUR** EARTH. AND OF COURSE THERE ARE LESS THAN A MILLION PEOPLE IN THE WHOLE SYSTEM. WE'VE ONLY BEEN SETTLED HERE FOR FIFTY YEARS -- SINCE 2380, OLD EARTH TIME.

IT'S A BEAUTIFUL SYSTEM -- SO PEACEFUL! OVER THIRTY HABITABLE PLANETS AND NOT A SERIOUS ENEMY... NOT UNTIL TODAY, THAT IS!

THAT'S *HIGH SIERRA,* THE ICE PLANET. NEXT STOP, *NEW EARTH!*

JUST LIKE OUR *MOON!* I'LL GO TELL THE DOCTOR WE'RE ALMOST THERE!

INTERESTING ...*VENOM DUCTS* IN BOTH CLAW AND FANG!

HMM! WONDER WHAT PROPERTIES IT HAS...DOESN'T SEEM TO HAVE AFFECTED ME--

GOOD LORD! MY HANDS!

WE'RE ALMOST AT NEW EARTH! DOCTOR --*WHAT'S* WRONG?

AIEEE!

NEXT WEEK: THE BEAST INSIDE!

19

DOCTOR WHO

and the DOGS of DOOM

ON THE ASTRO-FREIGHTER 'SPACEHOG' AN ATTACK BY WERELOK RAIDERS IS FOILED. BUT THE DOCTOR RECEIVES A SCRATCH FROM A WERELOK CLAW, AND LATER A FRIGHTENING CHANGE TAKES PLACE —

DOCTOR! WH--WHAT'S HAPPENED TO YOU?

PLEASE! DON'T HURT ME!

SCRIPT. MILLS & WAGNER ART. DAVE GIBBON

NRAAA!

ON THE FLIGHT DECK--

MERCY SAKES! THE BOW-WOW BOYS IS BACK!

DON'T SHOOT, MR BEAN! IT'S THE DOCTOR!

STAY AWAY FROM ME! CAN'T-- CONTROL MYSELF!

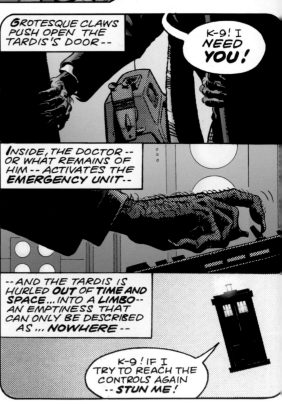

GROTESQUE CLAWS PUSH OPEN THE TARDIS'S DOOR--

K-9! I NEED YOU!

INSIDE, THE DOCTOR -- OR WHAT REMAINS OF HIM -- ACTIVATES THE EMERGENCY UNIT--

--AND THE TARDIS IS HURLED OUT OF TIME AND SPACE...INTO A LIMBO-- AN EMPTINESS THAT CAN ONLY BE DESCRIBED AS ...NOWHERE --

K-9! IF I TRY TO REACH THE CONTROLS AGAIN --STUN ME!

I'VE GOT A SAMPLE OF THE VENOM! THERE'S WORK TO BE DONE--

GOT TO FIGHT THIS THING--

FIGHT IT!

HE'S GONE!

POOR FELLA! MAYBE I SHOULDA JUST ZAPPED HIM--MIGHTA BEEN THE KINDEST THING!

IN THE TARDIS'S LAB, HOURS PASS--DAYS--AS THE DOCTOR STRUGGLES WITH THE BEAST INSIDE HIM--SEARCHING FOR THE ANTIDOTE--

ALL TOO OFTEN, THE BEAST TRIUMPHS!

NRRAAA!

--AND A BLACK, MURDEROUS VEIL SLIPS DOWN OVER THE DOCTOR'S MIND--

REGRET I MUST CARRY OUT YOUR INSTRUCTIONS, MASTER.

AFTERWARDS, THERE ARE ALWAYS THE SPELLS OF LUCIDITY...

NOT MUCH VENOM LEFT... CAN'T KEEP WASTING IT LIKE THIS!

PERHAPS THE DOCTOR'S OWN INHUMANITY SAVES HIM FROM THE FULL EFFECT OF THE VENOM--

OR PERHAPS HE IS PROTECTED BY SOME AS YET UNKNOWN POWER OF THE TARDIS...

BUT, AT LAST, A CURE IS FOUND--

IF THIS DOESN'T WORK--I'M DOOMED!

MASTER --YOU ARE WELL AGAIN.

AS WELL AS CAN BE EXPECTED, K-9-- I FEEL LIKE I'VE BEEN DRAGGED THROUGH A VELUSIAN TORTURE WHEEL!

THE TARDIS RE-APPEARS--

YOU MUST BE REALLY BRILLIANT, DOCTOR! YOU'VE ONLY BEEN GONE TEN MINUTES AND YOU'VE FOUND A CURE!

TEN MINUTES! MY DEAR GIRL --I'VE BEEN AWAY NEARLY *THREE MONTHS!*

TWO HOURS LATER, THE 'SPACEHOG' REACHES NEW EARTH --

BELOW, SYSTEM PRESIDENT WILSON K. WILSON IS WAITING--

APART FROM THE ATTACK ON YOUR SHIP, WE'VE LOST CONTACT WITH TWO OUTLYING PLANETS -- *DAVY CROCKETT* AND *LITTLE YUGOSLAVIA.* WE MUST ASSUME THEY'VE BEEN OVER-RUN. THESE CREATURES ARE POISONOUS, YOU SAY?

YES, THE VENOM APPEARS TO LIE DORMANT UNTIL THE BODY IS SUBJECTED TO LIGHT OF A CERTAIN INTENSITY--MOONLIGHT, SAY. I'VE GIVEN A SAMPLE OF THE ANTI-DOTE TO YOUR SCIENTISTS.

THIS WHOLE SYSTEM IS IN DANGER, MR PRESIDENT. I'VE GOT A FEELING YOU HAVEN'T EVEN *MET* YOUR REAL ENEMY YET!

LOOK AT THESE CREATURES. THEY'VE LITTLE MORE INTELLIGENCE THAN A PACK ANIMAL. THEY COULDN'T *CONTROL* THE TECH-NOLOGY WE'VE SEEN!

THEN *WHO*--

I'M JUST ABOUT TO FIND OUT! LEND ME YOUR CHAIN--THIS ONE IS COMING ROUND!

WATCH THE PRETTY CHAIN, BRILL--

UHHNN

YOU ARE GETTING SLEEPY... VERY SLEEPY... YOU CAN HARDLY KEEP THOSE HAIRY EYE-LIDS OPEN...

BRILL TALKS--

I BRILL, LEADER OF FORTY-NINTH WERELOK PACK. I TAKE ORDERS FROM FOUR-PACKER DRAKK--

GO ABOVE HIM, BRILL! TELL ME ABOUT YOUR BIG BOSSES. THERE ARE SOME WHO AREN'T OF YOUR RACE, AREN'T THERE?

YES, WE CALL THEM ...THE EVIL ONES! THEY ARE BAD -- MORE BAD THAN WERELOX. MAKE EVEN BRILL AFRAID.

THE EVIL ONES NOT LIKE LIVING THINGS -- THEY MORE LIKE ROBOT. MAKE WERE-LOX SERVE THEM. SAY EXTERMINATE! EXTERMINATE WHOLE SYSTEM!

NO! THAT WORD -- EXTER-MINATE!

WHAT IS IT, DOCTOR?

THE WORST NEWS POSSIBLE! YOU'RE DEALING WITH THE MOST EVIL RACE I HAVE EVER ENCOUNTERED ...THE DALEKS!

EXTERMINATE!

NEXT ISSUE THE DALEK MASTERS!

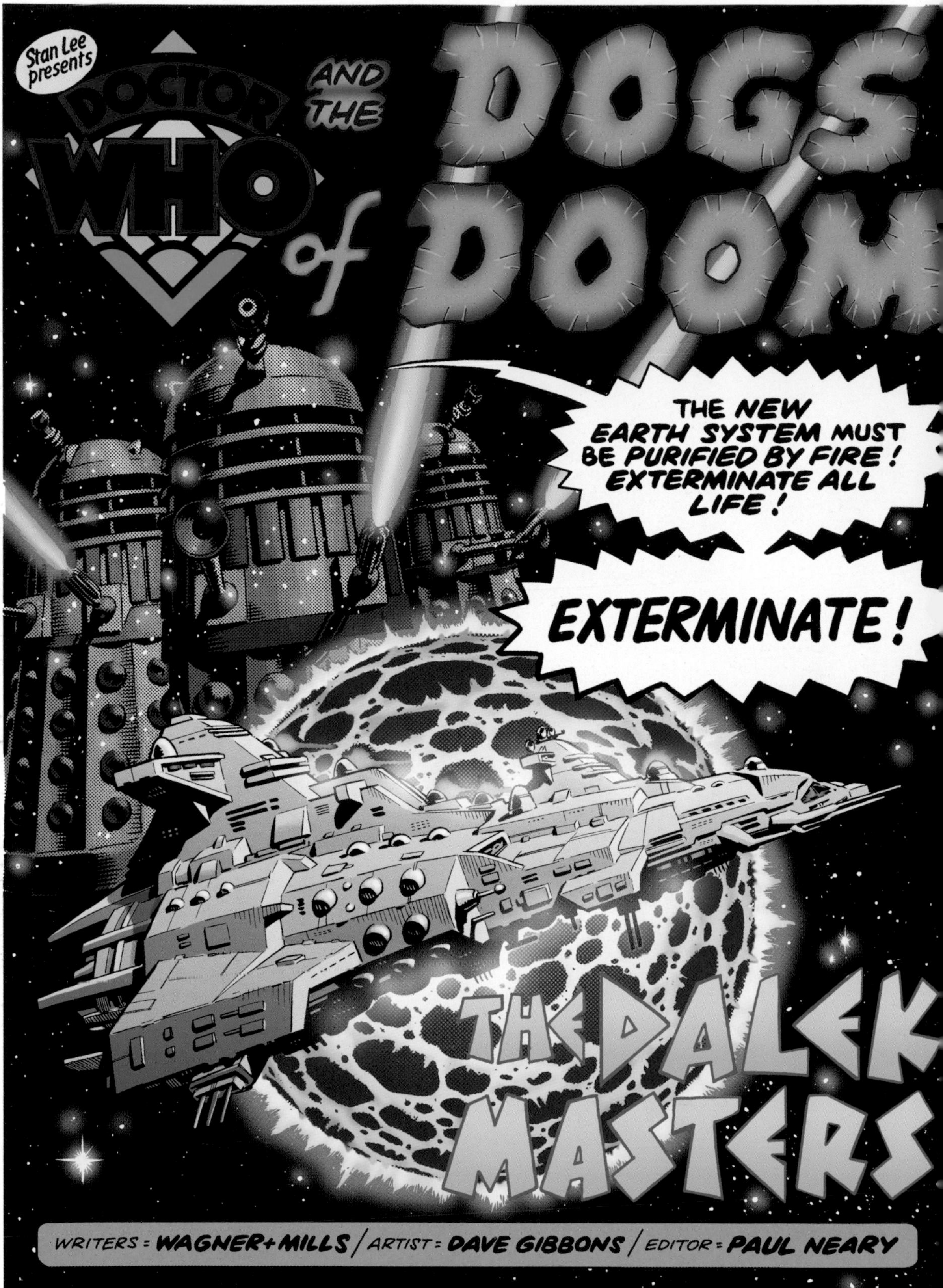

Stan Lee presents
DOCTOR WHO
AND THE
DOGS of DOOM
THE NEW EARTH SYSTEM MUST BE PURIFIED BY FIRE! EXTERMINATE ALL LIFE!
EXTERMINATE!
THE DALEK MASTERS
WRITERS = WAGNER+MILLS / ARTIST = DAVE GIBBONS / EDITOR = PAUL NEARY

THE PEACE OF THE DISTANT *NEW EARTH SYSTEM* HAS BEEN SHATTERED BY THE ARRIVAL OF A HUGE BATTLE-CRAFT CREWED BY *WERELOK STAR-SOLDIERS* AND THEIR EVIL MASTERS -- *THE DALEKS!*

THE *NEUTRON FIRE* IS EFFECTIVE! WHEN THE FLAMES HAVE DIED, THE PLANET WILL BE *STERILISED!* THEN THE *CLONING* CAN BEGIN!

NEUTRON FIRE DESTROYS ALL LIVING THINGS! WE NO LONGER NEED OUR *WERELOK SLAVES!*

THE WERELOX ARE EXTREMELY VICIOUS! THEY MAY STILL BE USEFUL TO US! BUT THEY NEED A LESSON IN *OBEDIENCE!*

GENERAL BOROX REPORTIN'! YOU SEND FOR ME, EVIL ONES?

YES! OPEN COMMUNICATIONS TO ALL PARTS OF THE SHIP!

ATTENTION! WERELOK SOLDIERS *FAILED* IN THEIR ATTACK ON THE HUMAN STARSHIP! THEREFORE, YOUR LEADER MUST BE PUNISHED!

HIS DEATH WILL BE SLOW AND PAINFUL! LET IT BE A WARNING! *OBEY US--*

OR ALL WILL BE EXTERMINATED!

AAAA! THE EVIL ONES HAVE NO MERCY!

AAAARROOO!

ON **NEW EARTH**, THE SYSTEM'S LARGEST PLANET, A DISTANT GLOW APPEARS IN THE SKY--

LOOK! IS IT A **METEOR**?

IS IT A **COMET**?

NO! IT-- IT'S **QUEEN VICTORIA**!

SCANNERS ZERO IN ON THE BLAZING PLANET--

IT'S **QUEEN VICTORIA**, ALL RIGHT, MR PRESIDENT! JUST A BALL OF FLAME!

WE'RE PICKING UP SIMILAR READINGS ON **NEW YUGOSLAVIA** AND **DAVY CROCKETT**! THE **DALEKS ARE DESTROYING THE SYSTEM PLANET BY PLANET!**

WE HAVEN'T THE WEAPONS TO RESIST THEM, DOCTOR! WE MUST **NEGOTIATE**!

DEAR ME, MR PRESIDENT, YOU CAN'T NEGOTIATE WITH **DALEKS**! THEY'RE HEARTLESS KILLERS WHO ONLY LIVE FOR POWER!

THEN **NEW EARTH** IS **DOOMED**!

THERE IS ONE CHANCE. A CLEVER MAN ON THE **INSIDE** MIGHT BE ABLE TO BEAT THEM...

BUT **HOW**?? **WHO**??

I HAVE THE **TARDIS**, AND I KNOW THE DALEKS-- NOT TO MENTION BEING ASTOUNDINGLY CLEVER ...REGRETTABLY, IT LOOKS LIKE I'M THE BEST MAN FOR THE JOB!

I'LL TAKE **BRILL** WITH ME. HE KNOWS THE DALEK SHIP.

THE **WERELOK**? CAN YOU TRUST HIM?

YES THANKS TO THE **HYPNOSIS**, HE THINKS HE'S ON **OUR SIDE** NOW!

SLASH, GO BRILL! BITE! CHOP! ALL DIE! AT **BATTLE OF DIRTY CLAW**, BRILL KILL THIRTY--NO, MORE! **TWENTY** MAYBE! NO WERELOK MORE BAD THAN BRILL!

COR! BRILL'S BEEN TELLING ME ALL ABOUT HIS BATTLES, DOCTOR! HE'S DONE SOME REALLY HORRIBLE THINGS!

AFFIRMATIVE, MASTER!

LET'S HOPE HE CAN DO SOME OF THEM TO THE DALEKS, BECAUSE THAT'S WHERE WE'RE GOING!

TAKE ME WITH YOU, DOCTOR!

NOT THIS TIME, SHARON. I'M AFRAID THERE'S A GOOD CHANCE I WON'T BE COMING BACK ALIVE!

SOON--

THERE GOES A BRAVE MAN!

CO-ORDINATES SET FOR THE DALEK SHIP! EVERYBODY READY?

BRILL ALWAYS READY, DOCTOR!

INTRUDER! INTRUDER ON CARGO DECK TWELVE!

EXTERMINATE THEM!

OH DEAR! I'D HOPED FOR A LITTLE BREATHING SPACE! K-9!

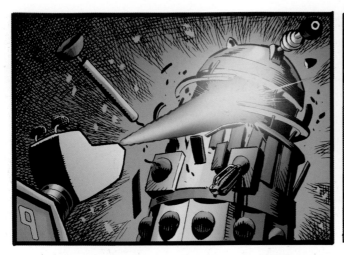

AAIIAAA! IT BRILL! BRILL OF THE FORTY NINTH!

WITH FRIGHTENING EFFICIENCY, BRILL METES OUT DEATH--

ENEMY WIPED OUT! WHO YOU WANT BRILL KILL NEXT?

COULD YOU PERHAPS START WITH THE PEANUT GALLERY UP THERE..?

THE EVIL ONES!

HELLO THERE! I'M AFRAID YOU'VE MISSED THE FIRST ACT! CAN YOU COME BACK TOMORROW?

EXTERMINATE!

I GUESS THAT MEANS NO!

NEXT: ALIEN ZOO!

DOCTOR WHO AND THE DOGS OF DOOM

THE DALEKS AND THEIR WERELOK HENCHMEN ARE ATTACKING THE NEW EARTH SYSTEM. THE DOCTOR, K-9 AND A TAME WERELOK, BRILL, USE THE TARDIS TO BOARD THE DALEK BATTLE CRAFT -- RIGHT INTO TROUBLE!

EXTERMINATE!

RUN!

NO! BRILL FEAR EVIL ONES, BUT BRILL NEVER RUN!

AAIAA! MAYBE RUN JUST THIS ONCE!

THIS DOOR'S LOCKED!

THAT IS *ROOM OF MANY CENTURIES!* IT IS *FORBIDDEN* -- EVEN TO OTHER EVIL ONES!

IT SEALED FROM INSIDE! EVIL ONES IN THERE NEVER COME OUT -- *NEVER!*

HEAVY SECURITY, EVEN FOR DALEKS! INTERESTING!

DALEKS CLOSING IN, MASTER!

DEAR ME! WHATEVER ELSE YOU MIGHT SAY ABOUT THEM, THEY'RE PERSISTENT!

THERE OTHER WAY! COME!

I WILL DELAY THEM, MASTER!

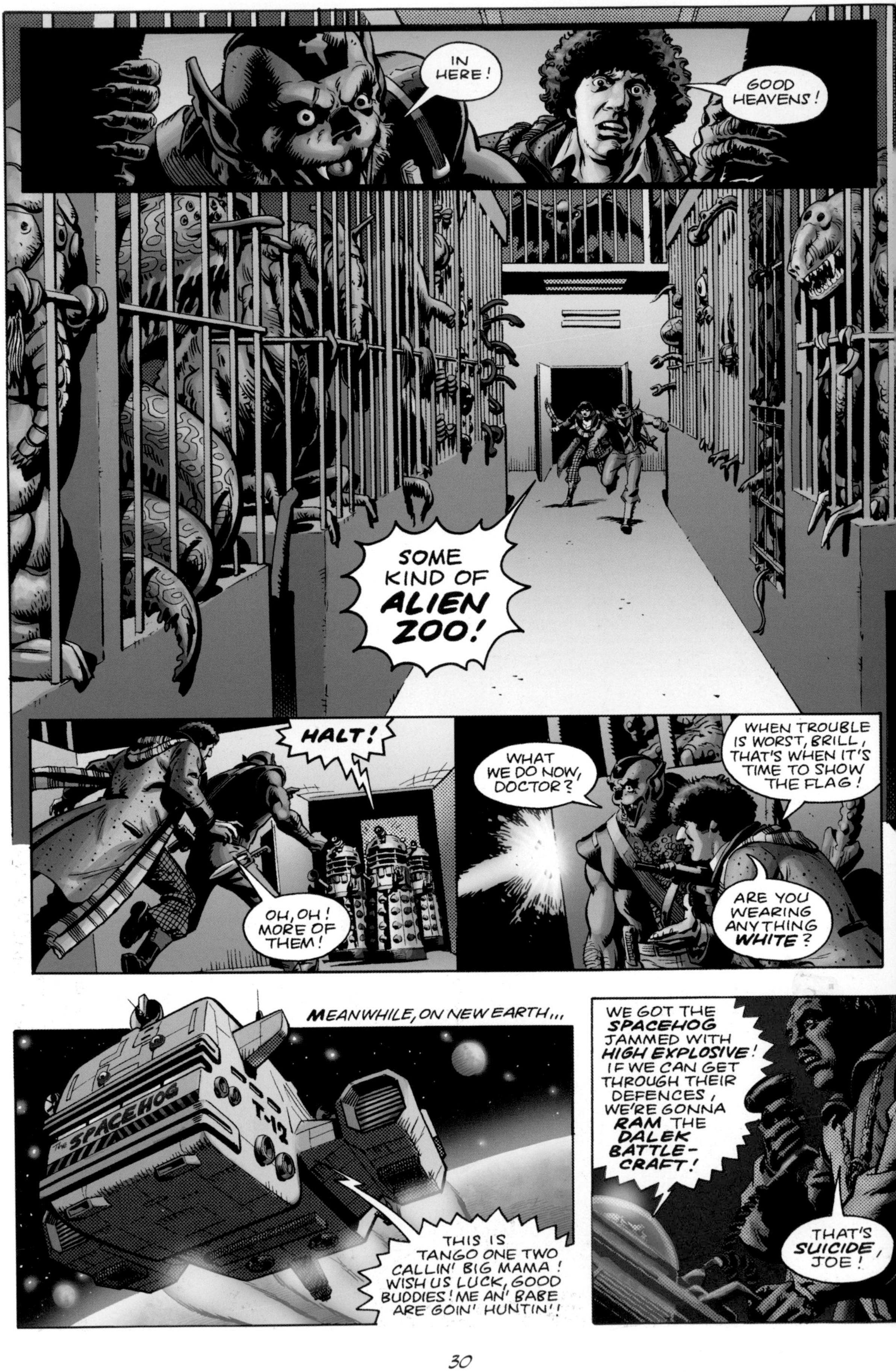
IN HERE!
GOOD HEAVENS!
SOME KIND OF ALIEN ZOO!
HALT!
OH, OH! MORE OF THEM!
WHAT WE DO NOW, DOCTOR?
WHEN TROUBLE IS WORST, BRILL, THAT'S WHEN IT'S TIME TO SHOW THE FLAG!
ARE YOU WEARING ANYTHING WHITE?
MEANWHILE, ON NEW EARTH...
THE SPACEHOG
T-12
THIS IS TANGO ONE TWO CALLIN' BIG MAMA! WISH US LUCK, GOOD BUDDIES! ME AN' BABE ARE GOIN' HUNTIN'!
WE GOT THE SPACEHOG JAMMED WITH HIGH EXPLOSIVE! IF WE CAN GET THROUGH THEIR DEFENCES, WE'RE GONNA RAM THE DALEK BATTLE-CRAFT!
THAT'S SUICIDE, JOE!

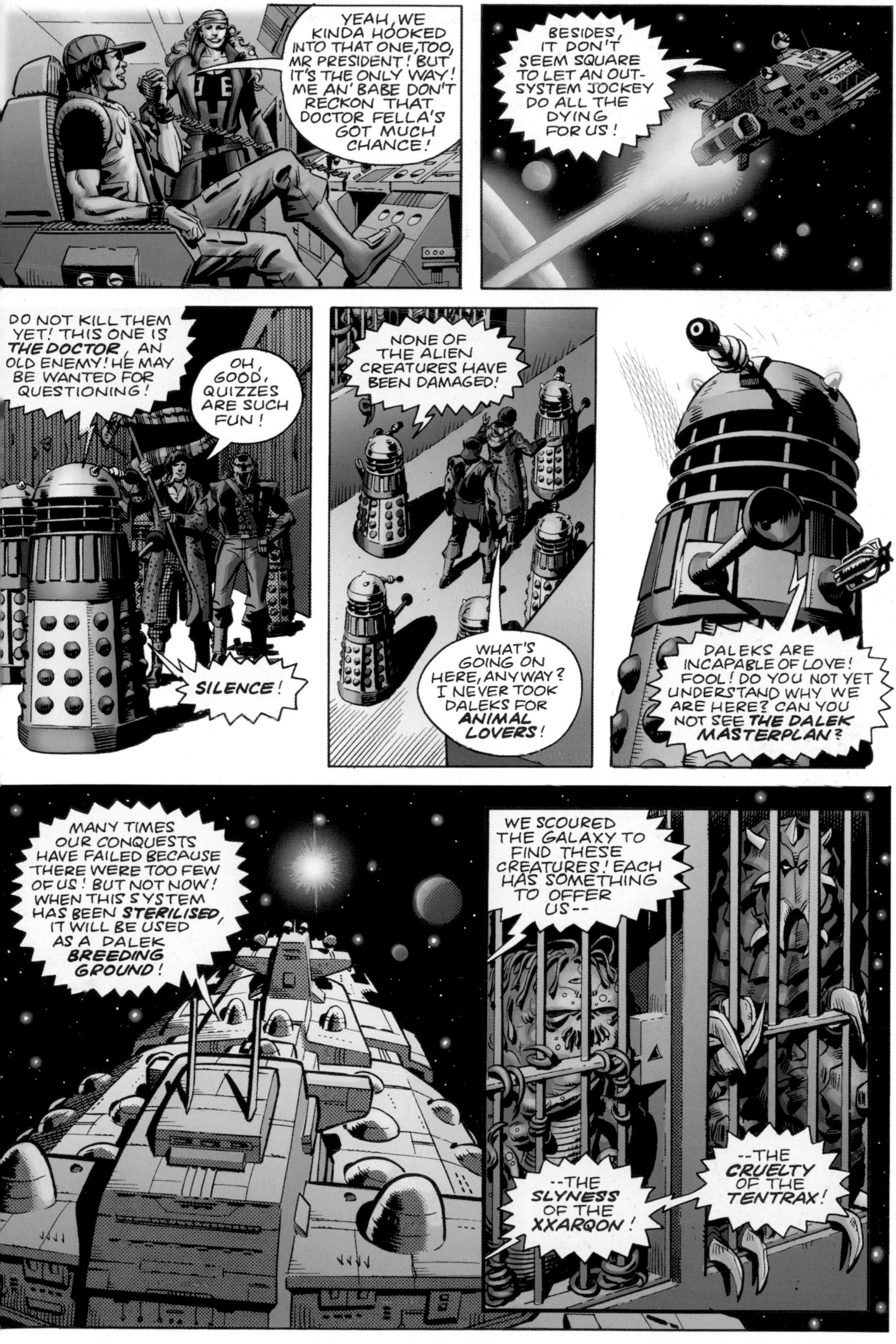
YEAH, WE KINDA HOOKED INTO THAT ONE, TOO, MR PRESIDENT! BUT IT'S THE ONLY WAY! ME AN' BABE DON'T RECKON THAT DOCTOR FELLA'S GOT MUCH CHANCE!
BESIDES, IT DON'T SEEM SQUARE TO LET AN OUT-SYSTEM JOCKEY DO ALL THE DYING FOR US!
DO NOT KILL THEM YET! THIS ONE IS THE DOCTOR, AN OLD ENEMY! HE MAY BE WANTED FOR QUESTIONING!
OH, GOOD, QUIZZES ARE SUCH FUN!
SILENCE!
NONE OF THE ALIEN CREATURES HAVE BEEN DAMAGED!
WHAT'S GOING ON HERE, ANYWAY? I NEVER TOOK DALEKS FOR ANIMAL LOVERS!
DALEKS ARE INCAPABLE OF LOVE! FOOL! DO YOU NOT YET UNDERSTAND WHY WE ARE HERE? CAN YOU NOT SEE THE DALEK MASTERPLAN?
MANY TIMES OUR CONQUESTS HAVE FAILED BECAUSE THERE WERE TOO FEW OF US! BUT NOT NOW! WHEN THIS SYSTEM HAS BEEN STERILISED, IT WILL BE USED AS A DALEK BREEDING GROUND!
WE SCOURED THE GALAXY TO FIND THESE CREATURES! EACH HAS SOMETHING TO OFFER US--
--THE SLYNESS OF THE XXARQON!
--THE CRUELTY OF THE TENTRAX!

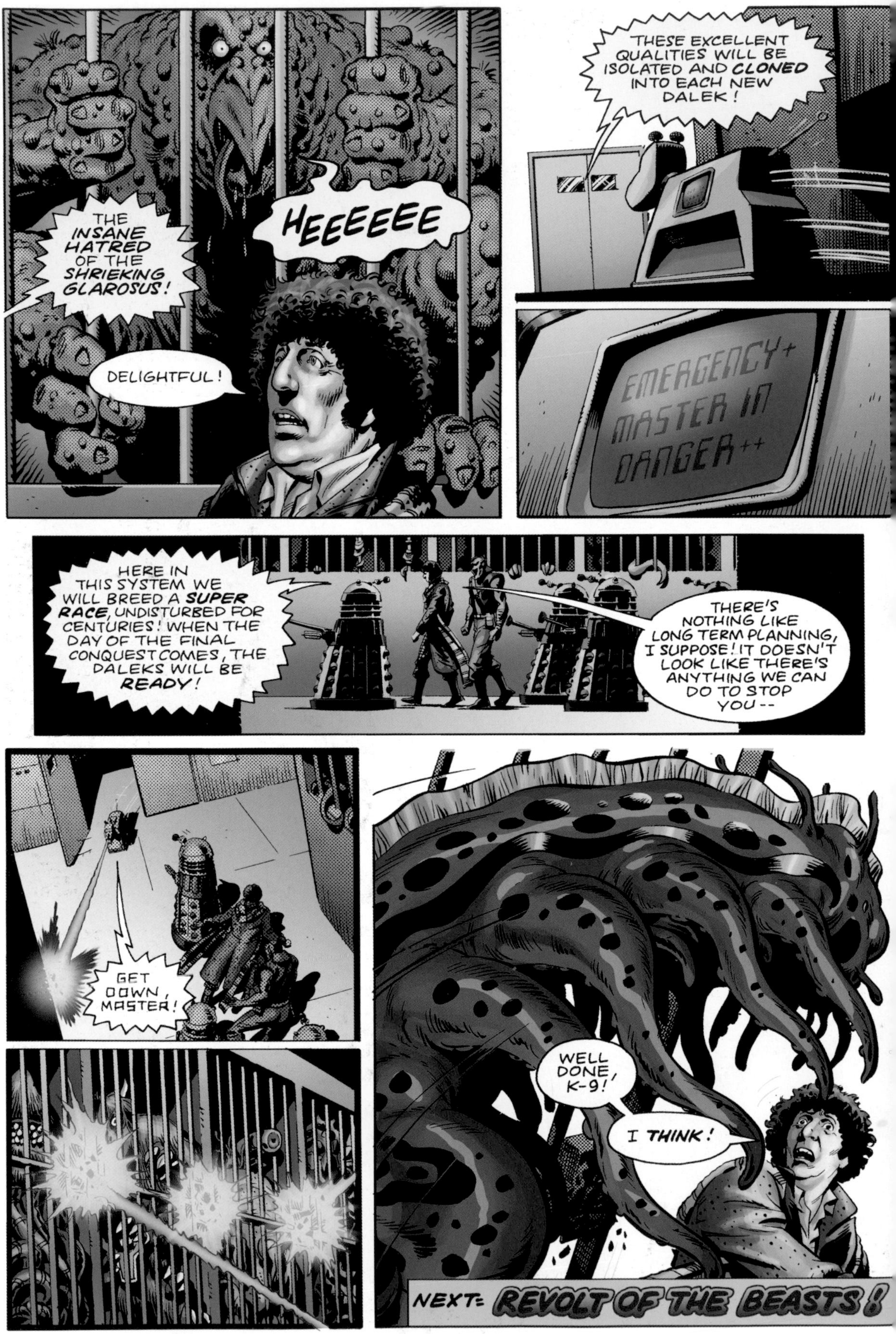
THE INSANE HATRED OF THE SHRIEKING GLAROSUS!
HEEEEEE
DELIGHTFUL!
THESE EXCELLENT QUALITIES WILL BE ISOLATED AND CLONED INTO EACH NEW DALEK!
EMERGENCY+ MASTER IN DANGER++
HERE IN THIS SYSTEM WE WILL BREED A SUPER RACE, UNDISTURBED FOR CENTURIES! WHEN THE DAY OF THE FINAL CONQUEST COMES, THE DALEKS WILL BE READY!
THERE'S NOTHING LIKE LONG TERM PLANNING, I SUPPOSE! IT DOESN'T LOOK LIKE THERE'S ANYTHING WE CAN DO TO STOP YOU--
GET DOWN, MASTER!
WELL DONE, K-9!
I THINK!
NEXT: REVOLT OF THE BEASTS!

DOCTOR WHO
and the DOGS of DOOM

THE DALEKS AND THEIR WERELOK HENCHMEN ARE ATTACKING THE NEW EARTH SYSTEM. SPACE TRUCKERS JOE BEAN AND BABE ROTH PREPARE TO RAM THE DALEK BATTLECRAFT IN A DESPERATE SUICIDE MISSION. BUT —

MASTER!

IT'S GOING FOR THE DALEK!

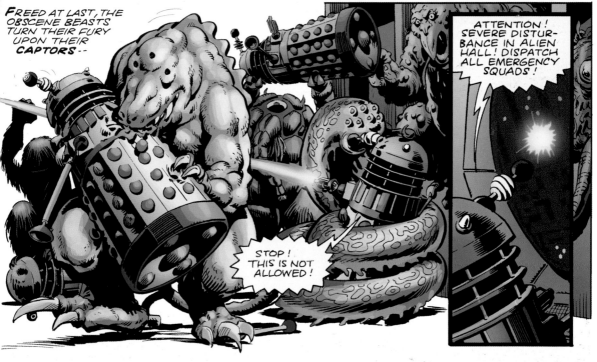

FREED AT LAST, THE OBSCENE BEASTS TURN THEIR FURY UPON THEIR CAPTORS --

STOP! THIS IS NOT ALLOWED!

ATTENTION! SEVERE DISTURBANCE IN ALIEN HALL! DISPATCH ALL EMERGENCY SQUADS!

OPENING MORE CAGES, MASTER!

THE MORE THE MERRIER, K-9!

ALL THE SAME, MAYBE WE SHOULDN'T PRESS OUR LUCK! LET'S GET MOVING!

BUT, IN THE CARGO DECK--

EMERGENCY SQUADS! WE NOT GET FAR, DOCTOR!

STAND BY, MRS ROTH. I HAVE A PERSON TO PERSON *VIDEO* FROM LUTINE BELL, NEW EARTH...

HEY, MA, IS IT *TRUE*? ARE YOU AN' JOE BEAN REALLY GONNA ATTACK THE *DALEK SHIP*?

PLEASE, MA, DON'T DO IT! YOU'LL BE KILLED!

YES... I'M AFRAID WE WILL...

I HAVE TO DO IT... IF JOE AND I DON'T GET THROUGH, THEN IT'S NOT JUST US--IT'S *YOU*, YOUR *FRIENDS--EVERYONE WE LOVE*! THE DALEKS WILL DESTROY *EVERYTHING*!

PLEASE, DARLINGS, TRY TO BE BRAVE...

BENSON! YOU LOOK AFTER THEM, YOU HEAR! MAKE SURE THEY'RE ALWAYS CLEAN AND WELL-BEHAVED-- AND KEEP FILBERT AWAY FROM THAT *SHUGGY HALL*!

YES, MRS ROTH. AND MAY I SAY, THE MEMBERS OF THE *LUTINE BELL ROBOSERVANTS CLUB* WILL BE HOLDING A SPECIAL MEMORIAL DINNER TO HONOUR WHAT YOU ARE DOING! THANK YOU... AND GOODBYE.

MEANWHILE--

YOU! HALT!

PRETEND I'M YOUR PRISONER, BRILL!

I TAKIN' THESE PRISONER FOR TORTURE, EVIL ONE!

STAND ASIDE SO YOU MAY BE RECOGNISED!

NRRAAAH!

ONE OF THE ALIENS!

SUBDUE IT! USE YOUR NET GUNS, YOU FOOLS!

NRAAAA!

I'D LOVE TO STAY, BUT I'M IN RATHER A HURRY TO GET TO MY TORTURE!

WHAT..? UH, YEAH, THAT RIGHT! BRANDIN' IRONS PROB'LY GETTIN' COLD!

EXTER-MINATE THEM!

GOT TO GET TO THE TARDIS --HURRY!

THEY'VE LEFT GUARDS!

ONLY THREE! BRILL TAKE 'EM WIT' ONE CLAW!

FOR BRILL, FEARED PACK LEADER OF THE FESTERING FORTY NINTH, THE GUARDS ARE CHILD'S PLAY--

WHAT'S HAPPENING, K-9? I CAN'T BRING MYSELF TO LOOK!

YOU ARE WISE, MASTER! IT IS NOT PLEASANT!

INSIDE-- OKAY, DOCTOR, HOW YOU WANT IT? 'LECTRIC SHOCK? BONE BREAKING? TORTURE OF MANY CUTS? BRILL KNOW 'EM ALL!

TORTURE? GOOD HEAVENS! THAT WAS ALL JUST A JOKE, BRILL!

JOKE, HUH? THAT NO FAIR! NOW YOU GOT BRILL ALL DISAPPOINTED!

LISTEN, BRILL! THAT SEALED ROOM--THE ONE YOU CALLED THE ROOM OF MANY CENTURIES --I SAW TIME TRAVEL EQUIPMENT IN THERE...

YES -- EVIL ONES BRING US HERE FROM MANY YEARS AGO! BUT ROOM IS LOCKED

THERE'S NO SUCH THING AS A LOCKED ROOM TO THE TARDIS!

I'VE GOT A PLAN! IF I CAN GET AT THAT TIME EQUIPMENT, WE CAN BEAT THE DALEKS!

THAT THERE DALEK BOOM BOOM BUGGY'S COMIN' UP ON SCAN! SHOOT ME THAT MOOSE JUICE, BABE!

YOU'RE JUICED, GOOSE!

WHEN WE HIT THEM SHIELDS, WE'LL BE TOUCHIN' TOES WITH TITAN! WE'LL BLOW THEM METAL MONKEYS HALFWAY TO HOTSIDE!

NEXT: BYE BYE, GOOD BUDDY?

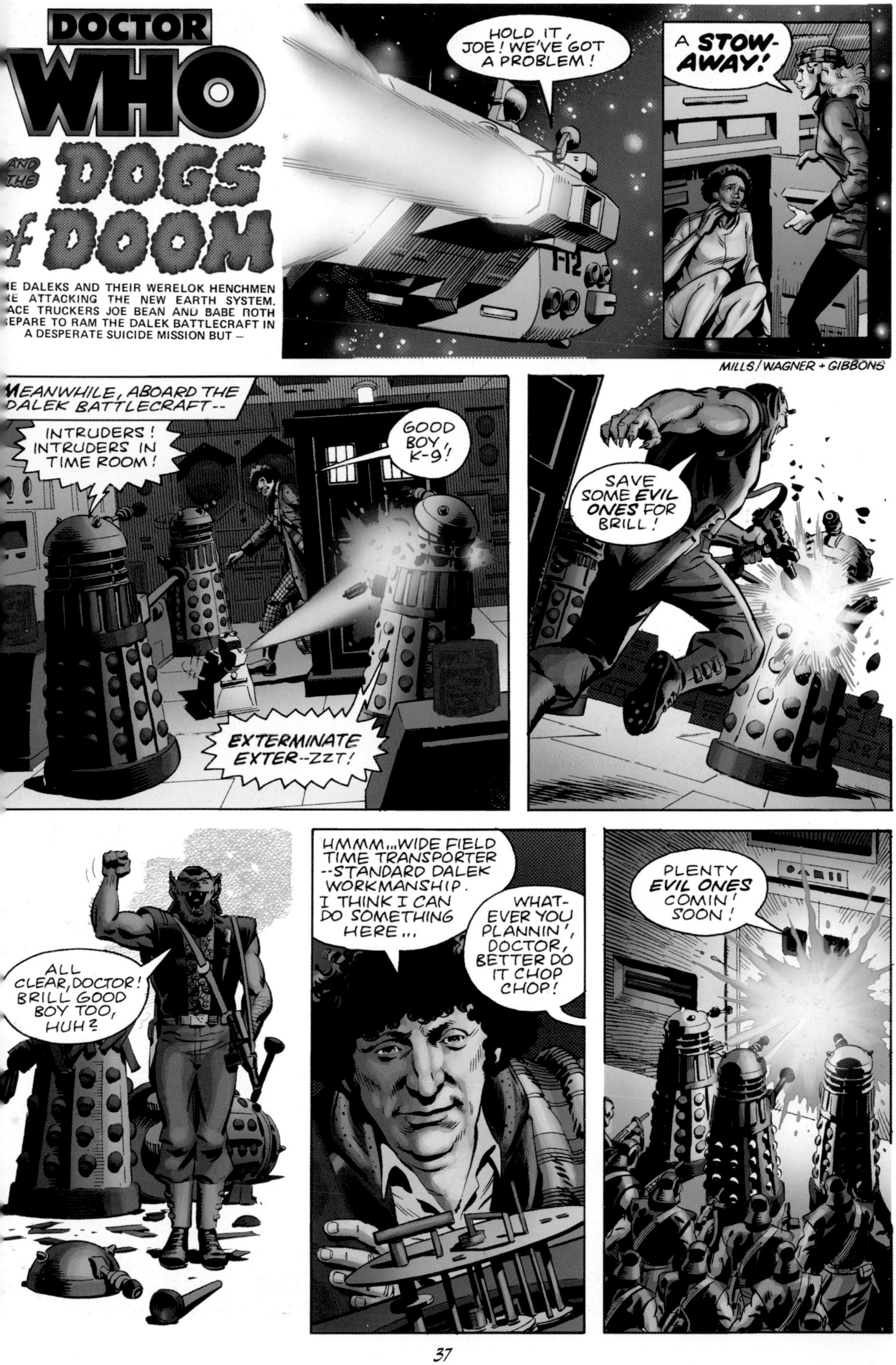
DOCTOR WHO AND THE DOGS of DOOM
HE DALEKS AND THEIR WERELOK HENCHMEN RE ATTACKING THE NEW EARTH SYSTEM. ACE TRUCKERS JOE BEAN AND BABE ROTH EPARE TO RAM THE DALEK BATTLECRAFT IN A DESPERATE SUICIDE MISSION BUT –
HOLD IT, JOE! WE'VE GOT A PROBLEM!
T-12
A STOW-AWAY!
MILLS/WAGNER + GIBBONS
EANWHILE, ABOARD THE DALEK BATTLECRAFT--
INTRUDERS! INTRUDERS IN TIME ROOM!
GOOD BOY K-9!
EXTERMINATE EXTER--ZZT!
SAVE SOME EVIL ONES FOR BRILL!
ALL CLEAR, DOCTOR! BRILL GOOD BOY TOO, HUH?
HMMM...WIDE FIELD TIME TRANSPORTER --STANDARD DALEK WORKMANSHIP. I THINK I CAN DO SOMETHING HERE...
WHAT-EVER YOU PLANNIN', DOCTOR, BETTER DO IT CHOP CHOP!
PLENTY EVIL ONES COMIN' SOON!

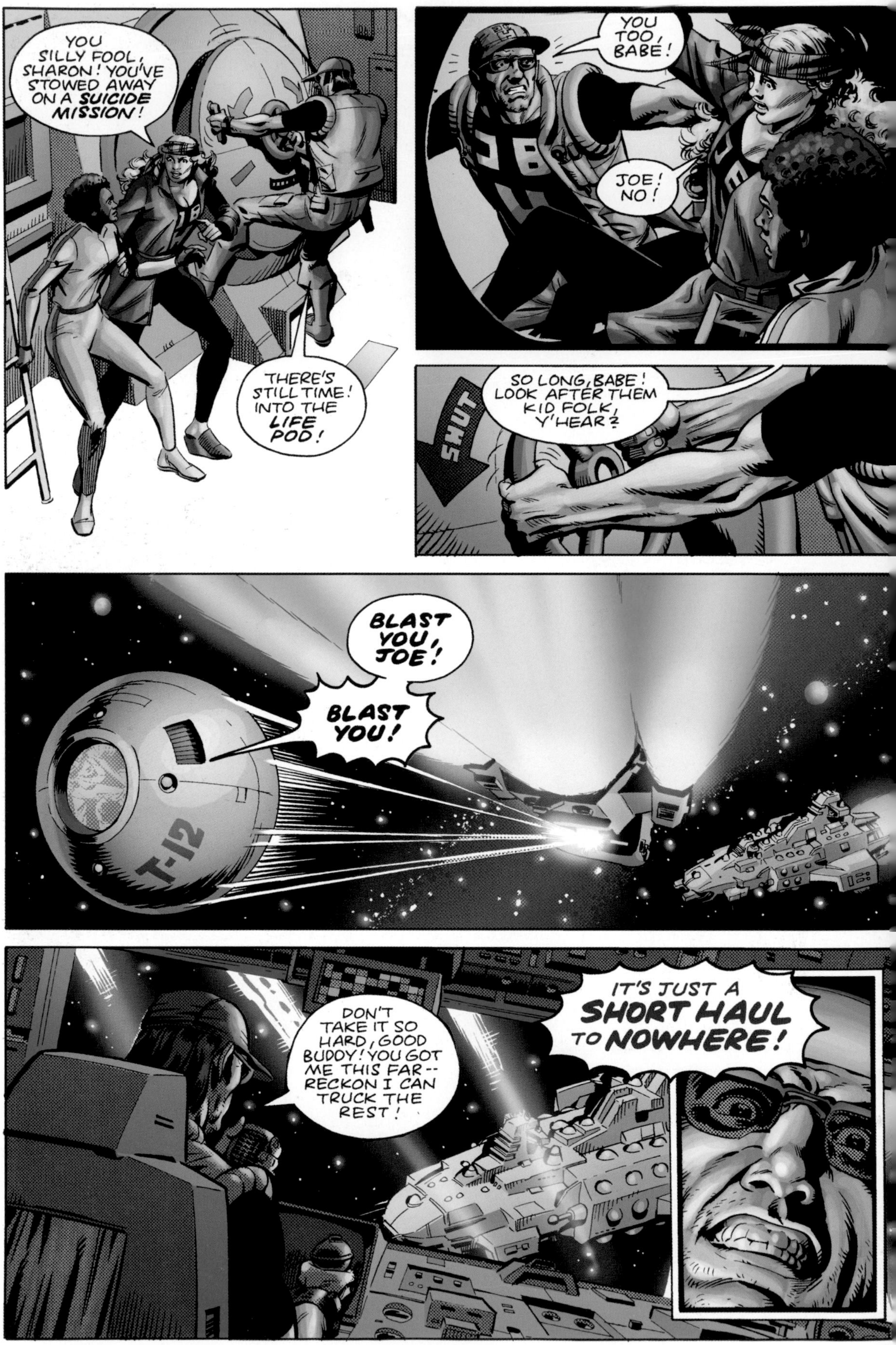
YOU SILLY FOOL, SHARON! YOU'VE STOWED AWAY ON A SUICIDE MISSION!
THERE'S STILL TIME! INTO THE LIFE POD!
YOU TOO, BABE!
JOE! NO!
SHUT
SO LONG, BABE! LOOK AFTER THEM KID FOLK, Y'HEAR?
BLAST YOU, JOE!
BLAST YOU!
T-12
DON'T TAKE IT SO HARD, GOOD BUDDY! YOU GOT ME THIS FAR-- RECKON I CAN TRUCK THE REST!
IT'S JUST A SHORT HAUL TO NOWHERE!

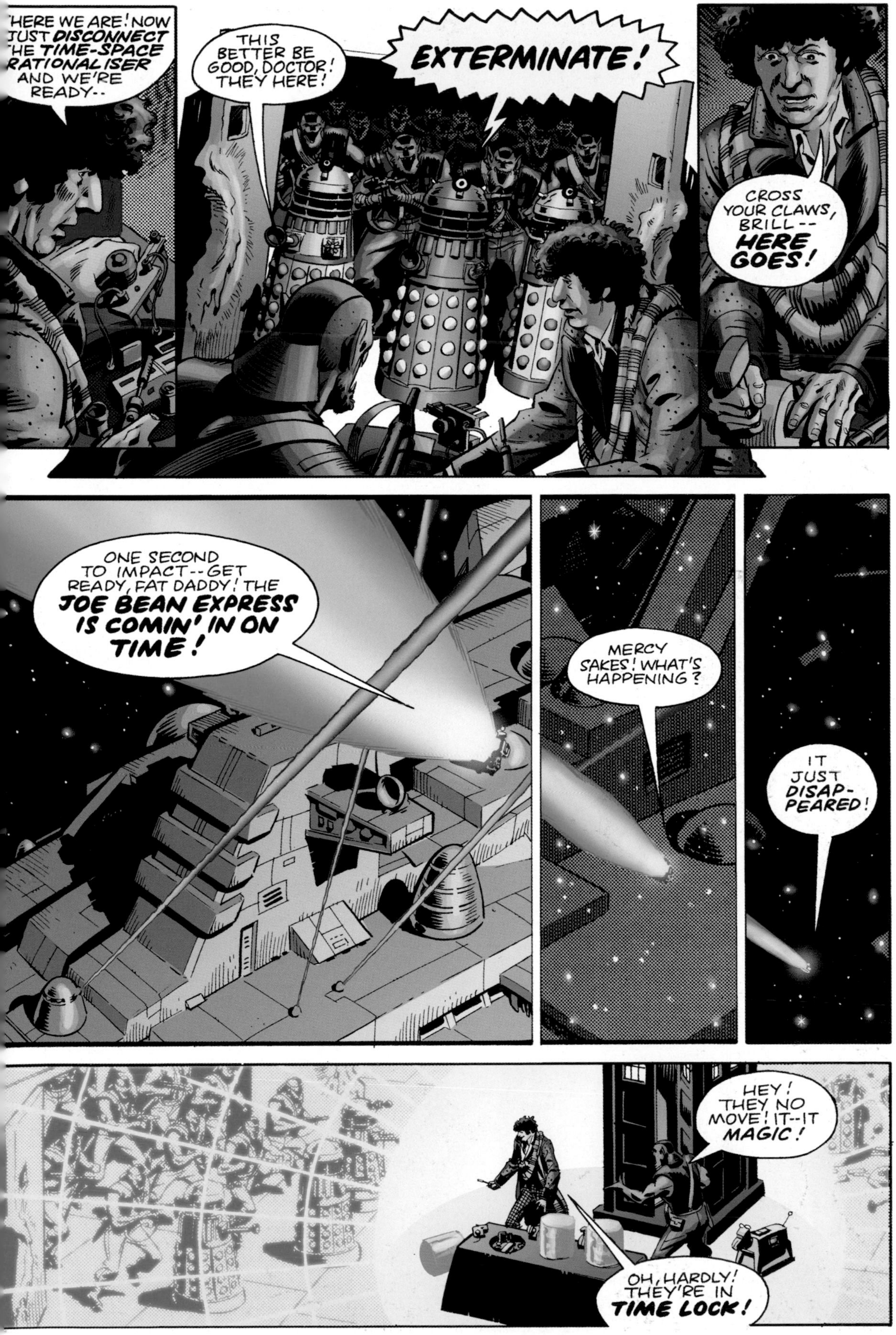
THERE WE ARE! NOW JUST DISCONNECT THE TIME-SPACE RATIONALISER AND WE'RE READY--
THIS BETTER BE GOOD, DOCTOR! THEY HERE!
EXTERMINATE!
CROSS YOUR CLAWS, BRILL -- HERE GOES!
ONE SECOND TO IMPACT--GET READY, FAT DADDY! THE JOE BEAN EXPRESS IS COMIN' IN ON TIME!
MERCY SAKES! WHAT'S HAPPENING?
IT JUST DISAP-PEARED!
HEY! THEY NO MOVE! IT--IT MAGIC!
OH, HARDLY! THEY'RE IN TIME LOCK!

THE ENTIRE SHIP IS LOCKED ON *ONE MOMENT* IN *TIME AND SPACE*! THEY'RE FROZEN IN THAT MOMENT --*FOREVER*!

WE CAN MOVE INSIDE THE *TIME VORTEX*. DON'T *TRY* TO STEP OUTSIDE IT!

SURE *SEEM* LIKE MAGIC!

MY DEEDS OFTEN HAVE THAT EFFECT-- COME ON--TIME WE WERE GOING!

SOON, ON NEW EARTH--

JOE BEAN HAS PICKED UP SHARON AND BABE ROTH. HE'S STILL WONDERING HOW THE DALEK SHIP DISAPPEARED!

TELL HIM HE MISSED IT -- BY A FRACTION OF A SECOND!

AND LATER--

BRILL STAY HERE ON NEW EARTH, DOCTOR! MAYBE JOIN ARMY--TEACH THESE SKINFACES HOW A WERE-LOK FIGHTS!

I PITY THE MEN IN YOUR PLATOON! WELL, SHARON, I REALLY MUST GET YOU BACK HOME...!

AW, DOCTOR, WHAT'S THE RUSH? I'M HAVING FUN! BESIDES, IF YOU'RE SO CLEVER, YOU CAN SET ME DOWN AN HOUR BEFORE I *LEFT*, THEN NOBODY'LL NOTICE I'VE BEEN GONE!

BETTER STILL, SET ME DOWN *TWO WEEKS* BEFORE I LEFT, AND I CAN GIVE MY DAD A BIG WIN ON THE *POOLS*!

I THINK WE'RE GOING TO HAVE PROBLEMS WITH THIS GIRL, K-9!

AFFIRMATIVE, MASTER!

THE END

NEXT ISSUE THE DOCTOR, SHARON AND K-9 MEET THE... TIME WITCH!

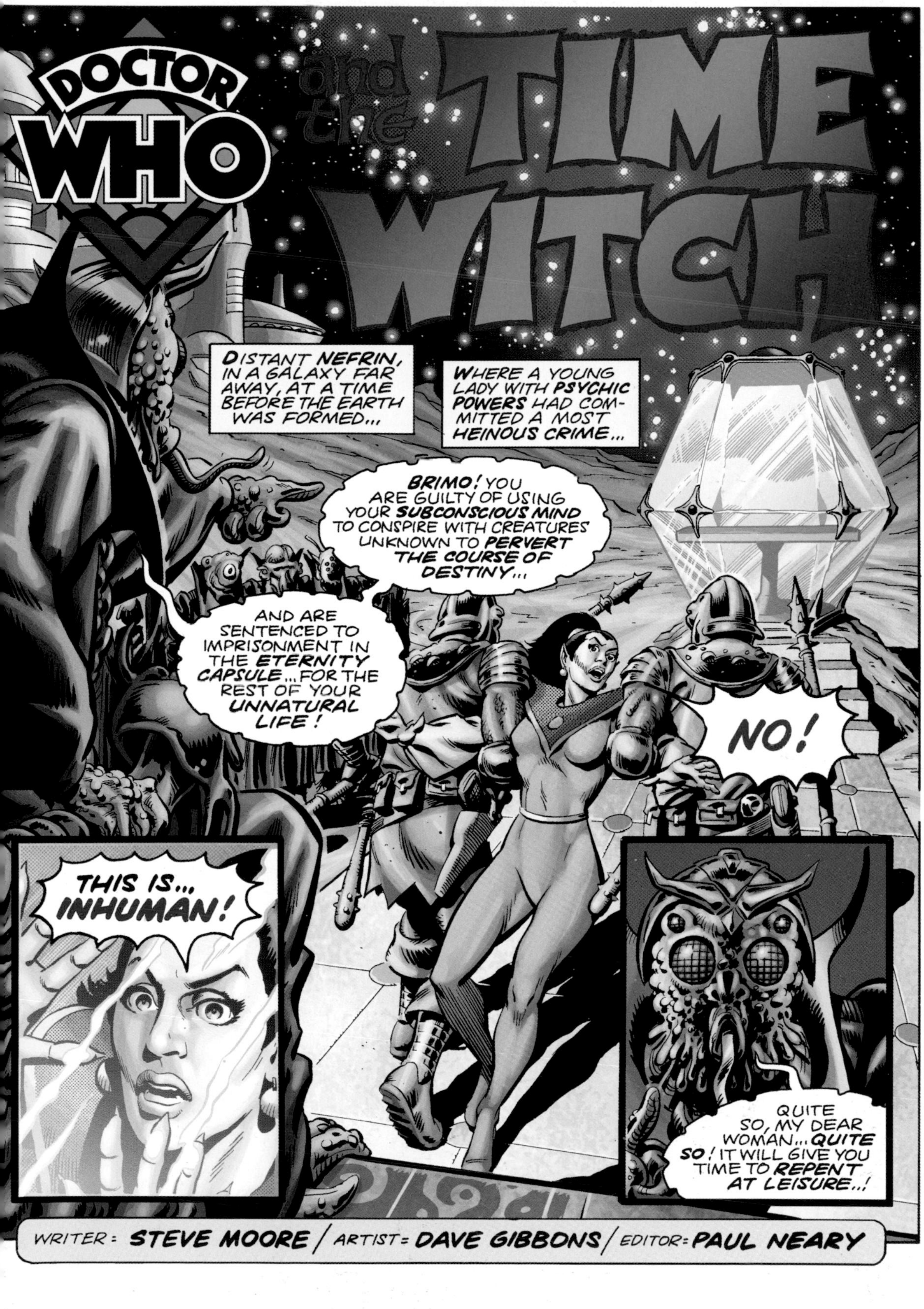
DOCTOR WHO
and the TIME WITCH
DISTANT NEFRIN, IN A GALAXY FAR AWAY, AT A TIME BEFORE THE EARTH WAS FORMED...
WHERE A YOUNG LADY WITH PSYCHIC POWERS HAD COMMITTED A MOST HEINOUS CRIME...
BRIMO! YOU ARE GUILTY OF USING YOUR SUBCONSCIOUS MIND TO CONSPIRE WITH CREATURES UNKNOWN TO PERVERT THE COURSE OF DESTINY...
AND ARE SENTENCED TO IMPRISONMENT IN THE ETERNITY CAPSULE... FOR THE REST OF YOUR UNNATURAL LIFE!
NO!
THIS IS... INHUMAN!
QUITE SO, MY DEAR WOMAN... QUITE SO! IT WILL GIVE YOU TIME TO REPENT AT LEISURE...!
WRITER= STEVE MOORE / ARTIST= DAVE GIBBONS / EDITOR= PAUL NEARY

ETERNAL IMPRISONMENT: TO WATCH AS EMPIRES WAX AND WANE, NATIONS CLEAVE ASUNDER AND COALESCE...

WHILE THE PATIENT WINDS, WITH UNTHINKING SKILL, GRIND DOWN **MOUNTAINS** INTO SEAS OF **SAND**...

UNTIL EVEN THE PLANET NEFRIN IS NOTHING MORE THAN A **MEMORY,** SLIPPING AWAY INTO THE TAIL-STREAM OF TIME...

SUCH IS THE **BOREDOM** OF ETERNAL LIFE, THAT WHEN THE **SUN ITSELF GOES NOVA**...

...THERE IS NO-ONE WATCHING...

YET, WITHIN ONLY A FEW MILLION YEARS, THE ANCIENT STAR HAS COLLAPSED INTO A **BLACK HOLE**...

AND THE **GRAVITIC WARPING** SUCKS BRIMO, FULLY AWAKE, INTO...

...**NOTHING.**

NOW WHERE IN THE NAME OF NEFRIN AM I?

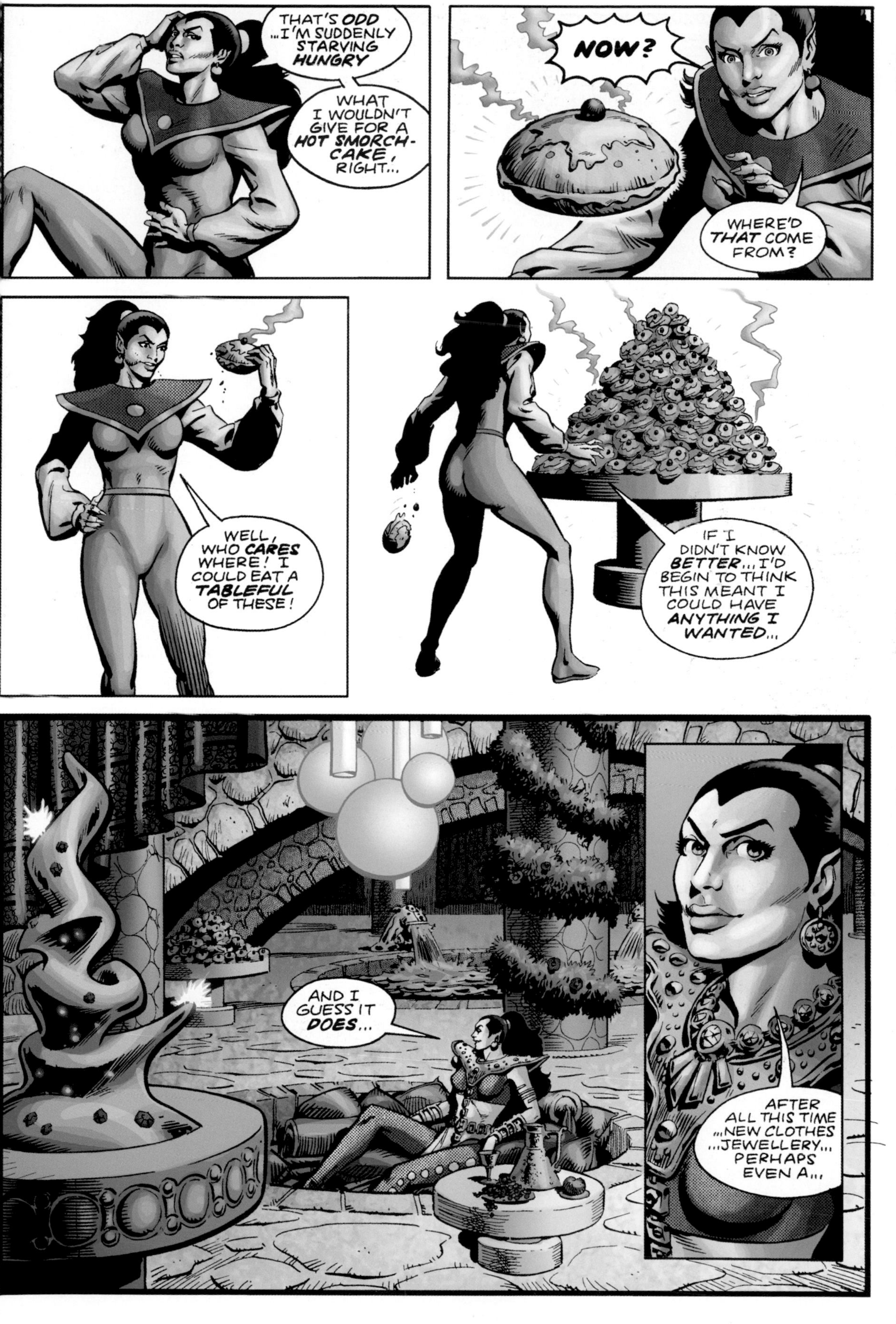
THAT'S ODD ...I'M SUDDENLY STARVING HUNGRY
WHAT I WOULDN'T GIVE FOR A HOT SMORCH-CAKE, RIGHT...
NOW?
WHERE'D THAT COME FROM?
WELL, WHO CARES WHERE! I COULD EAT A TABLEFUL OF THESE!
IF I DIDN'T KNOW BETTER... I'D BEGIN TO THINK THIS MEANT I COULD HAVE ANYTHING I WANTED...
AND I GUESS IT DOES...
AFTER ALL THIS TIME ...NEW CLOTHES ...JEWELLERY... PERHAPS EVEN A...

NEW HAIR-STYLE! LIKE IT, DOCTOR? WON'T RECOGNISE ME WHEN I GET BACK TO SCHOOL, WILL THEY?

DON'T SUPPOSE THEY WILL, SHARON... I HARDLY RECOGNISE YOU NOW!

STILL, UNTIL I CAN PERSUADE THE TARDIS TO TAKE YOU BACK TO BLACKCASTLE, YOU'LL BE MISSING CLASSES... PERHAPS WE SHOULD DO SOMETHING ABOUT THAT...

OH, COME ON, DOCTOR ...DON'T BE AN OLD FOGEY!

OH, IT'S NOT THAT BAD! WITH THIS RETINAL IMPLANT VIDDY MACHINE... THE WHOLE AFFAIR WILL BE OVER IN A FEW MINUTES..!

THAT THING WON'T MESS UP ME NEW HAIRSTYLE, WILL IT?

PICKED THIS UP IN A LITTLE SHOP ON THE PLANET FLOGSTRUNE... OR WAS IT MOBELI-FOUR ...ANYWAY, WHAT DO YOU THINK?

SMASHING, DOCTOR! REALLY GOOD!

FUNNY... I DIDN'T THINK IT WAS THAT INTERESTING!

OH DEAR! THAT WAS SUPPOSED TO BE 'ADVANCED HIGH SCHOOL PHYSICS'...

NOT 'THE GALACTIC CRIME-FIGHTER'S NOTEBOOK'...!

AH, WELL, LET'S SEE WHERE THAT'S...

HELLO! WHAT'S THIS?

HOW DID *THAT* GET HERE, DOCTOR?

THAT'D TAKE ANOTHER *VIDDY-REEL* TO EXPLAIN...!

JUST *KEEP BACK*, SHARON!

IT'S A *SPLIT* IN THE *VERY FABRIC OF TIME* ITSELF!

AND THAT MEANS *SOMEONE, SOME-WHERE*, IS DOING *SOMETHING*...

THAT THEY REALLY *SHOULDN'T!*

THE TIME CONTINUUM RUPTURES, SPLITTING THE TARDIS IN TWO...

OOPS!

DOES THAT MEAN THERE'S A DUPLICATE *US* IN THE *OTHER* TARDIS?

WELL, AS THERE'S NO *K-9* IN *OUR* TARDIS, I GUESS *NOT*...

BUT THIS IS *SERIOUS*...

SOMEONE'S GOT INTO A *BLANK DIMENSION* ...AND THEY'RE *DRAWING ENERGY* THROUGH FROM *OUR* DIMEN-SION...

THE *ONLY TROUBLE* IS...

THEY'RE JUST LIKELY TO SUCK *US* THROUGH *TOO!*

DOCTOR!

NEXT ISSUE *INTO THE ABYSS!*

DOCTOR WHO
THE TIME WITCH

THE FABRIC OF TIME ITSELF HAS RUPTURED WITHIN THE TARDIS, AND THE DOCTOR HAS BEEN SUCKED THROUGH THE GAP INTO ANOTHER DIMENSION ...

MOORE + GIBBONS

OOF! SOME SORT OF SOLID GROUND HERE... BIT TOO SOLID FOR MY LIKING!

AND THEN...

OOWWW!

AH, THOUGHT YOU'D BE ALONG IN A MOMENT, SHARON! LOOKS LIKE WE'RE IN SOME SORT OF CAVERN...

AT LEAST WE'RE NOT REALLY HURT...

WASN'T VERY COMFORTABLE, THOUGH, WAS IT? I COULD DO WITH A NICE...

HMM....

OH, DEAR...

HELLO! WOULD YOU CARE FOR A CUP OF TEA?

GOSH, THAT'S JOLLY DECENT OF YOU, OLD CHAP! JUST WHAT I WAS THINKING OF...

DON'T MENTION IT ...THE IDEA JUST POPPED INTO MY HEAD...

I'M MELTRON, GUARDIAN OF THE GATEWAY...

THE OPENING TO THE OTHER DIMENSION, YOU MEAN?

BUT IF YOU'RE THE GUARDIAN WHY DIDN'T YOU ATTACK US WHEN WE CAME THROUGH?

HOW SHOULD I KNOW? I'M JUST A FIGMENT OF SOMEONE ELSE'S IMAGINATION...

AH, BUT WHOSE?

CALLS HERSELF BRIMO...

BRIMO!?!

NEVER HEARD OF HER...

BUT SPEAKING OF WHOM...

MMM...FEELS LIKE IT MUST BE MORNING ...AND SO IT IS...

HARDLY SURPRISING, REALLY! NOW, LET'S SEE...

I THINK I'LL HAVE TWO SUNS IN THE SKY TODAY...

AND MAYBE OVER THERE...

A FOREST!

MMM...THAT'S BETTER...

PLACE IS STARTING TO LOOK ALMOST FAMILIAR NOW...

AND TALKING OF THE FAMILIAR...

DOCTOR... THE TARDIS!

THE DIMENSIONAL GATE MUST BE MORE *POWERFUL* THAN I THOUGHT... IT'S TURNED THE TARDIS INSIDE OUT AND SUCKED IT THROUGH AS WELL!

MUST HAVE GIVEN THE RELATIVE DIMENSION COMPENSATOR A *HIDEOUS SKRUNCH* THOUGH, TURNING IT *OUTSIDE-IN* AGAIN!

BUT CAN'T WE USE IT TO *GET AWAY* IN?

WOULDN'T BE VERY *POLITE*, WOULD IT? NOT WHEN WE'VE BEEN OFFERED A *NICE CUP OF TEA*! SHALL WE GO, MELTRON?

BESIDES, I THINK I'D RATHER LEAVE THE TARDIS WHERE IT *IS*, FOR NOW...

MEANWHILE, NOT FAR AWAY...

STRANGE... THE TREES HAVE *STOPPED GROWING*! WHAT'S GONE WRONG?

SOMETHING MUST BE CUTTING ME OFF FROM MY ENERGY SOURCE...

BUT I PUT *MELTRON* THERE TO GUARD THE GATEWAY...

NOW LET'S SEE WHAT HE'S...

WHAT?!

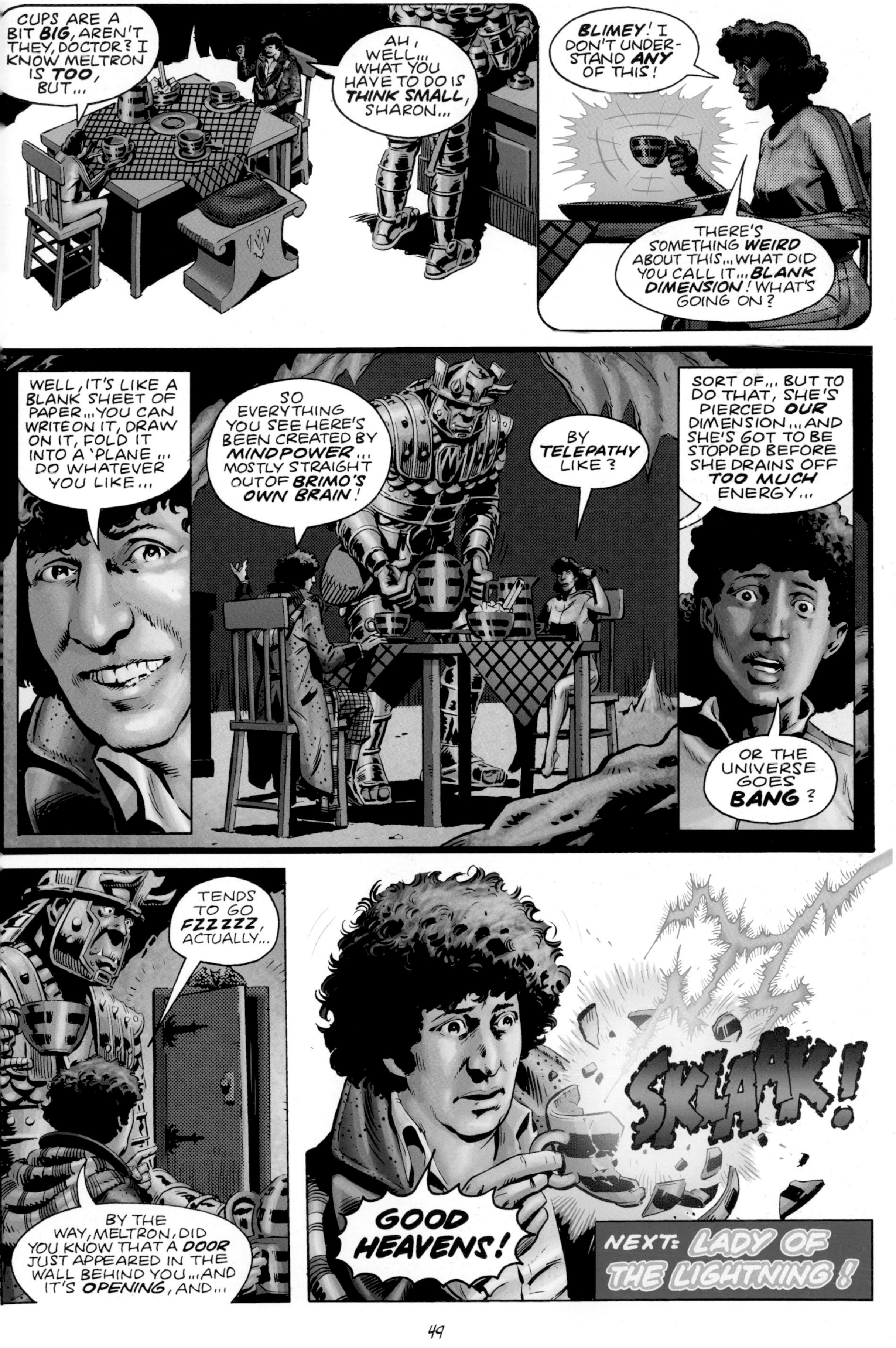

CUPS ARE A BIT BIG, AREN'T THEY, DOCTOR? I KNOW MELTRON IS TOO, BUT...
AH, WELL... WHAT YOU HAVE TO DO IS THINK SMALL, SHARON...
BLIMEY! I DON'T UNDER-STAND ANY OF THIS!
THERE'S SOMETHING WEIRD ABOUT THIS... WHAT DID YOU CALL IT... BLANK DIMENSION! WHAT'S GOING ON?
WELL, IT'S LIKE A BLANK SHEET OF PAPER... YOU CAN WRITE ON IT, DRAW ON IT, FOLD IT INTO A 'PLANE... DO WHATEVER YOU LIKE...
SO EVERYTHING YOU SEE HERE'S BEEN CREATED BY MINDPOWER... MOSTLY STRAIGHT OUT OF BRIMO'S OWN BRAIN!
BY TELEPATHY LIKE?
SORT OF... BUT TO DO THAT, SHE'S PIERCED OUR DIMENSION... AND SHE'S GOT TO BE STOPPED BEFORE SHE DRAINS OFF TOO MUCH ENERGY...
OR THE UNIVERSE GOES BANG?
TENDS TO GO FZZZZZ, ACTUALLY...
BY THE WAY, MELTRON, DID YOU KNOW THAT A DOOR JUST APPEARED IN THE WALL BEHIND YOU... AND IT'S OPENING, AND...
SKLAAK!
GOOD HEAVENS!
NEXT: LADY OF THE LIGHTNING!

DOCTOR WHO
THE TIME WITCH

THE DOCTOR AND SHARON HAVE BEEN SUCKED INTO A BLANK DIMENSION, WHERE BRIMO, THE TIME WITCH, HAS CREATED A WORLD WITH HER OWN MENTAL POWERS...

WHO ARE *YOU*? I DIDN'T THINK *YOU* UP!

OH, I DON'T KNOW... PERHAPS YOU DID ME IN AN *OFF-MOMENT*... OR PERHAPS YOU'VE *FORGOTTEN*...

MOORE + GIBBONS

I WOULDN'T HAVE DREAMED UP ANYONE SO *WEIRD*! AND I DIDN'T THINK OF *THESE*, EITHER!

WELL, NO... *I* DID...

YOU DID?

THEN THESE TWO MUST BE *PHYSICALLY REAL*, LIKE ME! AND THE MAN COULD BE *DANGEROUS*..!

ANYONE WHO CAN THINK FOR THEMSELVES CAN BE DANGEROUS IN *THIS* PLACE..!

LOOK OUT, SHARON!

YOUNG WOMAN! WILL YOU KINDLY STOP *DOING* THAT!

YOUNG? I'VE WATCHED *SUNS* GROW LEPROUS WITH AGE...WITHER ...DIE...

BUT *I'M* STILL HERE...

AND YOU SOON **WON'T** BE!

BOLTS OF **PURE** PSYCHIC ENERGY ...IT'S REALLY **VERY** INTERESTING!

BUT, DOCTOR... YOU'VE GOT TO **THINK** OF SOMETHING!

WELL, I'LL **TRY**...

AND, AS THE DOCTOR BEGINS TO **THINK** CREATIVELY...

HMM...NOT **QUITE** WHAT I WANTED, BUT IT'S **SOMETHING**, I SUPPOSE...

I WAS **TRYING** TO THINK OF **K-9**...

NOW **LISTEN**... CAN'T WE TALK THIS OVER?

IF THAT HAT WAS **REAL**, I'D START GETTING **UPSET** ABOUT THIS!

CAN'T **HIT** HIM... IT'S AS IF HE'S **WILLING** MY LIGHTNING TO MISS!

MELTRON! YOU CAN KILL THEM!

AS BRIMO'S GIANT THOUGHT FORM STUMPS FORWARD...

OH, **COME ON,** MELTRON! YOU DON'T WANT TO KILL ME!

HOW ABOUT **MAKING ANOTHER CUP OF TEA?**

KILL THEM!

MAKE A CUP OF TEA!

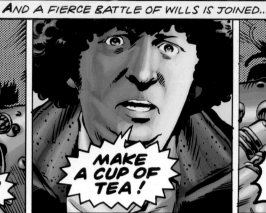

KILL THEM!

HMM...I SEEM TO BE TORN APART BY INNER CONFLICT...

OH DEAR! I'VE HEARD OF A *SPLIT PERSONALITY* ...BUT I DIDN'T THINK *THAT* WOULD HAPPEN...

KILL THEM!

MAKE A CUP OF TEA!

KILL THEM!

WOKK!

WHAT'S *HAPPENING*, DOCTOR?

MAKE A CUP OF TEA!

WOKK!

WELL, BY CONCEN-TRATING HARD, I THOUGHT I COULD THINK MELTRON INTO THINKING NICE THOUGHTS...

WOKK!

KILL THEM!

BUT I ONLY SEEM TO HAVE GOT THE JOB *HALF DONE!* I THINK THIS IS *STALE-MATE,* BRIMO...

SO WE MAY AS WELL GO AWAY AND LEAVE THEM TO IT!

GET YOUR HANDS OFF ME

WOK!!

MAKE A CUP OF TEA!

AH, SO THIS IS THE *MODEST LITTLE PALACE* YOU'VE THOUGHT UP FOR YOURSELF! BIT *EXTRAVAGANT* FOR ME, BUT...

HOLD ON, DOCTOR! HOW DID WE GET *HERE*? WE WERE *UNDERGROUND* A MOMENT AGO!

THERE'S NO *DISTANCE* BETWEEN HERE AND MELTRON'S PLACE...BECAUSE THERE *ISN'T ANYTHING* BETWEEN HERE AND THERE...

I SAID...

BRIMO HASN'T THOUGHT OF WHAT TO FILL THE SPACE WITH YET, HAVE YOU, BRIMO?

...*GET YOUR HANDS OFF!*

OOPS! WHAT A *TEMPER*!

DON'T TAKE ME *LIGHTLY*, YOU! *LOOK*! I CAN PUT *TWO SUNS* IN THE SKY! DON'T THINK I CAN'T HANDLE *YOU*!

ALL I'VE GOT TO DO IS *THINK*...

AND I CAN SUMMON UP AN *ARMY OF KILLERS*!!

NEXT: *MIND-TWIST!*

DOCTOR WHO
THE TIME WITCH

THE DOCTOR AND SHARON HAVE BEEN SUCKED INTO A BLANK DIMENSION RULED BY BRIMO, THE TIME WITCH, WHERE THOUGHT CAN CREATE A WORLD . . . OR AN ARMY OF KILLERS . . .

VERY IMPRESSIVE, BRIMO... BUT RATHER *SILLY*! ALL THAT EFFORT TO *CREATE* THEM ...

WHEN I *JUST* HAVE TO THINK OF A *HOLE IN THE FLOOR* TO GET RID OF THEM! *MUCH* EASIER!

HEY, DOCTOR, YOU'RE GETTING REALLY GOOD AT THIS *MIND-POWER* LARK!

WELL, PRACTICE MAKES PERFECT!

NOW, BRIMO, WHILE I THINK UP A FEW *STONE SLABS* TO KEEP THE UGLIES UNDER-GROUND ...YOU'LL NOTICE THE *SECOND SUN'S GONE OUT*..!

NO!

AH, BUT, *YES* ... THERE'S A *LIMIT* ON YOUR POWER-SOURCE NOW, BRIMO!

FIRST SUN'S GETTING A BIT *DIM*, TOO, ISN'T IT?

HOW COME, DOCTOR?

BECAUSE THE *TARDIS* IS STUCK IN THE DIMENSIONAL GATEWAY LIKE A *PLUG*, SHARON! THAT'S WHY I *LEFT* IT THERE!

WE'VE JUST GOT TO THINK OF THINGS TO *DEFEND* OURSELVES WITH UNTIL SHE RUNS OUT OF POWER...

SO NOW IT'S LIKE A GAME OF *CHESS*...

AND THE ONLY WAY SHE CAN CREATE SOMETHING *NEW* IS TO DESTROY SOMETHING *OLD*...

OOPS! A WHOLE *HILLSIDE* WENT THAT TIME, BRIMO!

DEFENCE IS *OKAY*, DOCTOR... BUT IF WE *ATTACK* AS WELL, WE'LL GET THIS OVER QUICKER!

NO, SHARON!

BLIMEY, DOCTOR, I...

I CAN'T *STAND* UP!

WON'T BE FOR LONG, SHARON!

BUT WHAT *NOW*, BRIMO? THERE'S *NOTHING LEFT* OUTSIDE THIS ROOM AFTER THAT!

I'LL THINK OF SOMETHING! I HAVEN'T BEEN LOCKED UP FOR MILLIONS OF YEARS JUST TO...

LOCKED UP? I *THOUGHT* THERE WAS SOME-THING *CRIMINAL* ABOUT YOU!

I WON'T FEEL SO BAD WHEN THIS IS OVER THEN...

STILL, YOU'VE ONLY GOT ENOUGH POWER FOR *ONE LAST THROW*, BRIMO... YOU'D BETTER MAKE IT *GOOD!*

WHAT'S THE MOST *TERRIFYING* THING YOU CAN THINK OF?

THE MOST TERRIFYING THING? THAT'S...

55

NO!!

NOT...

THE ETERNITY CAPSULE!

AND, AS THE DOCTOR'S TRAP IS SPRUNG...

NO, NOT AGAIN...*PLEASE*! THERE'S NO WAY OUT! I'LL BE TRAPPED IN HERE *FOR-EVER*!

THEN THAT SHOULD KEEP YOU OUT OF TROUBLE!

BYE, BYE, BRIMO!

MY CHAINS...*EVERY-THING*...THEY'VE ALL *FADED OUT*! THERE'S ONLY *US* LEFT!

US... AND THE *TARDIS*!

AT LEAST, *OUR* HALF OF IT! LET'S SEE IF IT CAN GET US OUT OF HERE!

WE WON'T HAVE TO WORRY ABOUT *BRIMO* ANY MORE... SHE HASN'T ENOUGH *POWER* LEFT TO GET OUT OF THAT THING...

BUT INSIDE, AFTER A QUICK CHECK...

OH, DEAR...THE SPLIT IN TIME'S WIDENED TO *FOUR YEARS* ACROSS! AND IT RUNS RIGHT THROUGH THE *CHRONO-COMPENSATOR*!

IT'S NOT GOING TO TAKE US *FOUR YEARS* TO GET BACK TO THE OTHER HALF OF THE TARDIS, IS IT?

NO, WE CAN DO IT *INSTANTLY*... BUT THE *EFFECT'S* THE SAME...

WELL, THERE'S NO WAY ROUND IT, SO...

THE DOCTOR THROWS THE SWITCH, AND...

HELLO, *K-9*! WE'RE *BACK*!

TARDIS RE-INTEG-RATED AND FUNCTIONING, MASTER!

DOES THAT MEAN YOU CAN GET ME BACK TO SCHOOL THEN, DOCTOR?

NOT A LOT OF *POINT* NOW, SHARON ...LET ME SEE, I THINK I'VE GOT A *MIRROR* HERE SOMEWHERE...

BLIMEY! I'VE SUDDEN-LY *GROWN* UP!

THAT'S WHAT I MEANT ABOUT THE *CHRONO-COMPENSATOR* NOT WORKING...WE'VE MADE THE TRIP IN AN *INSTANT*... BUT WE'VE BOTH *AGED FOUR YEARS*!

I SHALL STILL THINK OF MYSELF AS *743* ...OR WAS IT *730*, I NEVER CAN REMEMBER...

BUT FOR *YOU*, THE CHANGE IS A BIT MORE *NOTICEABLE*...

THEY WON'T *KNOW* ME WHEN I GET HOME...

LOOK ON THE BRIGHT SIDE, SHARON... SOME THINGS YOU'LL BE *GLAD* TO MISS OUT ON ...

NOW *ME*...I WAS A SPOTTY TEENAGER FOR *FIFTY* YEARS!

THE END.

NEXT ▷ JOIN THE DOCTOR, SHARON AND K-9 IN... **DRAGON'S CLAW!**

DOCTOR WHO
DRAGON'S CLAW

IT IS 1522 A.D., ACCORDING TO THE CALENDAR OF THE WESTERN-OCEAN-DEVILS, BUT FEW EUROPEANS ARE SEEN ON THE SHORES OF THE EAST CHINA SEA...

HERE IN CHEKIANG, THE FISHERMEN KNOW IT SIMPLY AS **THE YEAR OF THE PIRATE...**

THE SUMMER OF DEATH!

WRITER: **STEVE MOORE** / ARTIST: **DAVE GIBBONS** / EDITOR: **PAUL NEARY**

FOR YEARS, THE JAPANESE PIRATES HAVE BEEN RAVAGING THIS COAST, AND EVEN THE SOLDIERS OF THE NEW EMPEROR *CHIA-CHING* CAN DO NOTHING TO STOP THEM...

AAAYAAGH!

INDEED, IT SEEMS THAT *NO-ONE* CAN QUELL THEIR TYPHOON FURY...

MY BROTHERS ...MY *PARENTS* ... YOU ...!

THIS IS NOT A JOB FOR *SOLDIERS*...

GET YOUR HANDS OFF ME, YOU FILTHY DWARF!

*N*OR EVEN FOR *HEROES*...

?

GLERK!

THIS IS A TASK FOR THE *HOLY*!

A MONK!?!

TH-THANK YOU, MASTER...

SAY NOTHING, GIRL ...MISFORTUNES ARE MANY IN THIS SINFUL WORLD ...

BUT I HAVE HEARD THAT IF YOU READ THE SCRIPTURES, LEAD A HOLY LIFE ...

REPEAT THE BUDDHA'S NAME ...OBEY HIS COMMANDMENTS ...

WHAA...!

AND *DO NOT KILL*...

...YOU WILL SURELY ASCEND TO PARADISE WHEN YOU DIE ...

BUT THE MONK IS NOT ALONE, AND CLOSE AT HAND...

TOO MANY OF THE WOLVES SNAPPING AT MY HEELS...

AND THE **ABBOT YUEH KUANG** FINDS HIMSELF WITH A PROBLEM...

NO ALTERNATIVE ...BUT IF THERE'S NO ONE AROUND TO SEE...

...THERE'S NOTHING TO STOP ME USING THE **STAR WEAPON!**

YZZZAAK!

OOORGH!

YAAAGH!

BUT AS ABBOT YUEH MOVES AWAY TO REJOIN HIS MEN...

WELL, SHARON, WE'RE HERE...

THIS TIME IT'S **DEFINITELY** GOOD OLD **EARTH!**

BUT I'M NOT SURE WHEN...

OH, DOCTOR...

CAN'T WE JUST GET OUT OF HERE, DOCTOR?

NO, HOLD ON, SHARON...THERE'S SOMETHING STRANGE...

THIS MELTED HELMET...SOMEONE'S BEEN USING ENERGY WEAPONS! AND WHENEVER THIS IS, IT'S NOT TIME FOR THEM!

I THINK WE'D BETTER TAKE A LOOK AROUND...

BUT I CAN STILL HEAR FIGHTING IN THE DISTANCE!

JUST A QUICK LOOK... SEE WHAT WE CAN FIND...

WURK!

OOPS! SOMEONE'S FOUND US!

MORE PIRATES! A BLUE-EYED WESTERN DEVIL AND AN AFRICAN GIRL...

HOLD ON, MATE...I'M BRITISH!

AND I DON'T EVEN COME FROM THIS PLANET!

KILL THEM!

NEXT: MONASTERY OF MYSTERY!

61

DOCTOR WHO
DRAGON'S CLAW

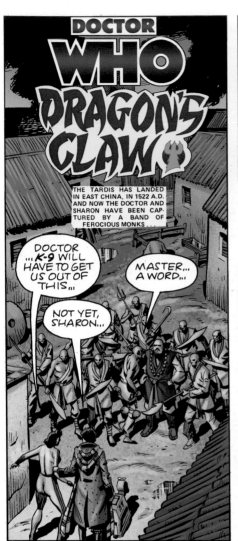

THE TARDIS HAS LANDED IN EAST CHINA, IN 1522 A.D. AND NOW THE DOCTOR AND SHARON HAVE BEEN CAPTURED BY A BAND OF FEROCIOUS MONKS...

DOCTOR...K-9 WILL HAVE TO GET US OUT OF THIS...

MASTER...A WORD...

NOT YET, SHARON...

THEIR ARRIVAL WAS MOST STRANGE...ONE MOMENT THERE WAS NOTHING...AND THEN...

AND WHEN THE TALE HAS BEEN TOLD...

THEY ALSO HAVE AN IRON DOG WHICH MOVES OF ITSELF...!

HMM...THE FOREIGN DEVILS ARE KNOWN TO BE CLEVER WITH THEIR HANDS...EVEN IF THEIR BEHAVIOUR IS BARBAROUS...

TAKE THEM WITH US...

WHY DIDN'T YOU USE K-9 TO STUN THEM, DOCTOR?

I'M KEEPING HIM IN RESERVE--UNTIL WE NEED A LITTLE SURPRISE...

WE DON'T NEED THAT NOW?

COURSE NOT! A NICE LITTLE CART-RIDE!

HOW FAR ARE WE GOING?

TO SUNG MOUNTAIN...A THOUSAND LEAGUES...

OH...

WELL, IN THAT CASE, WOULD YOU CARE FOR A...

"...JELLY BABY?"

"BLIMEY! IF YOU'RE *MONKS* ...HOW COME YOU'RE SO GOOD WITH *SWORDS*?"

"OUR MONASTERY HAS PRACTISED MARTIAL SKILLS FOR A *THOUSAND YEARS* ..."

"WE DO NOT *WISH* TO KILL... BUT SOME PEOPLE ARE SIMPLY *TOO OUTRAGEOUS*..."

"BESIDES, IF A VILLAIN IS FATED TO DIE UNDER MY SWORD, IT IS *DESTINY*, AND CANNOT BE HELPED..."

"WATCH FOR PIRATE STRAGGLERS, BROTHER LI..."

"AND YOU ... WHO ARE *YOU*?"

"THIS IS *SHARON*... AND I'M THE *DOCTOR*..."

"A DOCTOR?"

"ARE YOU A *HERBALIST*? A *NEEDLER*? A *BONE-SCRAPER*?"

"WELL, NO... MORE A DOCTOR OF THE *MIND*, ACTUALLY..."

"THE MIND? HOW DO YOU MAKE A HOLE IN THE PATIENT'S HEAD TO OPERATE?"

"NO IT'S NOT LIKE *THAT*, EITHER..."

AND SO THE JOURNEY NORTH-WEST CONTINUES THROUGHOUT THE DAYS THAT FOLLOW, BROKEN ONLY BY RIGOROUS PRACTICE-SESSIONS AT DAWN AND DUSK ...

"I SAY, YOU CHAPS ARE REALLY *AWFULLY GOOD*!"

"TOO RIGHT!"

THANK YOU ...BUT THESE ARE ONLY THE *SIMPLER* OF THE EXERCISES TAUGHT BY THE EIGHTEEN BRONZE MEN...

BRONZE MEN? NOW WHO COULD *THEY* BE, I WONDER?

IT IS NOT PERMITTED TO DISCUSS SUCH MATTERS, BROTHER CHANG...

ESPECIALLY WITH THE FOREIGN DEVILS...

HMM...FIRST *ENERGY WEAPONS* ...NOW *'BRONZE MEN'*...AND LI OBVIOUSLY WANTS TO KEEP SOMETHING *WELL-COVERED*...

BUT PERHAPS WE'LL FIND OUT MORE WHEN WE GET WHERE WE'RE GOING...

THEN FINALLY, ONE MORNING, THE SUNG MOUNTAIN AND...

THE SHAOLIN MONASTERY!

COO! IT'S BEAUTIFUL

BUT, ONCE WITHIN THE MONASTERY WALLS...

I DON'T THINK MUCH OF THIS SMELLY OLD STOREROOM THEY'VE PUT US IN, DOCTOR!

I THINK IT'S PROBABLY THE BEST THAT CAN BE EXPECTED, SHARON...

...FOR A PAIR OF *PRISONERS!*

NEXT: *THE OLD MAN OF THE MOUNTAINS!*

DOCTOR WHO

DRAGON'S CLAW

CHINA, 1522 A.D.: THE DOCTOR AND SHARON HAVE BEEN CAPTURED BY A BAND OF FEROCIOUS MONKS AND TAKEN TO THE SHAOLIN MONASTERY. AFTER BEING HELD PRISONER FOR SEVERAL HOURS...

IT'S NEARLY *DARK*, DOCTOR ...AND HE *STILL* HASN'T MOVED HE *MUST* BE ASLEEP BY NOW...

WE COULD WALK OUT PAST HIM...

I DON'T THINK WE *COULD* SHARON...

I'LL SHOW YOU...

OFF YOU GO, K9...A STRAIGHT LINE, AND STOP IF YOU COME TO AN OBSTRUCTION...

HE'S GOING TO MAKE IT, DOCTOR... I *TOLD* YOU CHANG WAS ASLEEP...!

THA AK

OBSTRUCTION, MASTER!

YOU ARE *WISE*, DOCTOR ...BETTER TO LOSE AN *IRON DOG* THAN YOUR *LIFE*

PERHAPS THE *ABBOT* COULD TELL US ABOUT THE MONASTERY'S HISTORY?

QUITE RIGHT! STILL, IT WOULD BE NICE TO LOOK ROUND THE PLACE...

ABBOT YUEH HAS BEEN HERE ONLY EIGHT YEARS... AND DEVOTES HIS TIME TO *MARTIAL MATTERS*...

YOU WOULD WANT TO SPEAK TO THE HERMIT, *HSIANG THE ANCIENT*...

ONCE *HE* WAS ABBOT HERE ...BEFORE HE TOOK TO MEDITATION, UP THERE IN THE HILLS...

HE COULD TELL YOU ALL YOU DESIRE...BUT ALAS, YOU CANNOT SEE HIM...

OH, BUT I THINK WE *CAN*...

STUN HIM, K-9!

AWFULLY SORRY, OLD BEAN...

FORGOT TO TELL YOU MY IRON DOG *BITES!*

THEN...

HAVE TO LEAVE YOU BEHIND, K-9...

DON'T TELL ANY-ONE WHERE WE'VE GONE!

COME ON, DOCTOR...

UP THIS WAY ...THAT'S WHERE CHANG WAS POINTING...

THAT WAS *EASY*...THEY MUST ALL BE ASLEEP ALREADY...

AND, BEFORE LONG...

HELLO! *HSIANG THE ANCIENT*, I PRESUME!

BLIMEY! HE'S BURIED UP TO THE WAIST!

WHEN THE INTRODUCTIONS HAVE BEEN MADE...

THE EARTH? THE WINDS BLOW IT TO ME, SO WHY SHOULD I BRUSH IT AWAY? AT LEAST IT'S NOT AUTUMN... THEN THE *LEAVES*...

DON'T YOU *EVER* MOVE?

NOT SINCE *YUEH KUANG* ARRIVED FROM MOUNT OMEI...

'...AND THE MONKS OF MOUNT OMEI HAVE ALWAYS BEEN RUMOUR-ED TO PRACTICE *HERETICAL MAGIC*...

'SO PERHAPS *HE* HAD SOMETHING TO DO WITH THE *STAR-FALL* THAT HAPPENED SOON AFTER HE ARRIVED...

'HE DISAPPEARED FOR THREE MONTHS... THEN RETURNED TO DEMONSTRATE A NEW SKILL HE HAD MASTERED...

'HE CALLED IT THE *STYLE OF THE EIGH-TEEN BRONZE MEN*, BUT I ONLY EXPERIENCED IT *ONCE*...

'AND *THEN* I DID *NOT* SEE THE BLOW...'

SINCE WHEN I'VE BEEN MEDITATING HERE... THEY BRING ME FOOD WHEN I FALL ASLEEP, BUT YOU'RE THE FIRST *REAL* PEOPLE I'VE SPOKEN TO IN *EIGHT YEARS*!

YOU *ARE* REAL, AREN'T YOU? YOU LOOK SORT OF... *FUNNY*...

YES, THEY'RE *REAL*, YOU OLD FOOL! AND WHEN THE ABBOT DISCOVERS THEY TRIED TO ESCAPE THE MONASTERY...

...THEY'LL DIE A *REAL DEATH*!

NEXT ISSUE: **SONTARANS!**

DOCTOR WHO
DRAGON'S CLAW

CHINA, 1522 AD.. THE DOCTOR AND SHARON HAVE BEEN CAPTURED BY FEROCIOUS MONKS FROM THE SHAOLIN MONASTERY. ESCAPED TO TALK TO THE HERMIT, HSIANG THE ANCIENT, THEY ARE DISCOVERED...

ON YOUR FEET, FOREIGN DEVIL!

I SAY, YOU REALLY ARE BEING RATHER *UNREASONABLE*, YOU KNOW!

RIGHT! YOU'VE GOT...

NOW, SHARON!

WHA...?

... NO *MANNERS* AT ALL, INTERRUPTING LIKE THAT!

UUH...

ZIK!

YOUNG PEOPLE UNDER SIXTY GOT NO *RESPECT* THESE DAYS! WHOLE *WORLD'S* GOING TO PIECES!

HE KNOCKED HIM OUT WITH JUST A *TOUCH*, DOCTOR!

NOW'S OUR CHANCE TO GET *OUT* OF HERE!

NO... IF THE FIRST THING LI OPENS HIS EYES TO IS THE OLD MAN, HE COULD GET A BIT *NASTY*...

WE'LL HAVE TO GET HIM AWAY FROM HERE...

YOU DON'T MEAN ... *CARRY* HIM?

YOU *DID* MEAN CARRY HIM! HE'S *HEAVY*, DOCTOR... COULDN'T WE GET RID OF THE *CHAIN*?

AH NO, I'VE GOT SOMETHING IN MIND FOR THAT...

SEE YOU LATER, OLD FELLA! DON'T GO AWAY!

AND, SOME DISTANCE AWAY...

THERE...THAT MIGHT HOLD HIM... FOR A *MINUTE OR TWO* ANYWAY...

BUT I HOPE WE'RE *GONE* WHEN HE WAKES UP!

GONE *WHERE*, DOCTOR?

BACK TO THE MONASTERY, OF COURSE!

BACK TO THE *MONASTERY*?

THINK OF IT, SHARON... *ENERGY WEAPONS, STAR-FALLS, BRONZE MEN*...THERE'S A *MYSTERY* HERE...

AND THE ONLY PLACE WE'LL FIND THE ANSWER ...IS BACK IN THE MONASTERY...

BESIDES, YOU DON'T WANT TO WALK FOUR HUNDRED MILES BACK TO THE TARDIS, DO YOU?

BUT WHAT HAPPENS WHEN *LI* GETS BACK?

FIRST WE'VE GOT TO WORRY ABOUT WHAT HAPPENS WHEN *WE* GET BACK!

BUT...

CHANG'S STILL *STUNNED*, DOCTOR...

GOOD! WE'LL JUST PRETEND *NOTHING* HAPPENED...

HELLO, K-9!

UH... HOW DID I GET DOWN HERE ON THE FLOOR?

FELL ASLEEP, OLD CHAP! HAPPENS TO *EVERYONE* SOONER OR LATER...

ASLEEP? **MOST** STRANGE!

BUT I AM SURPRISED YOU DID NOT **ESCAPE**!

WHO... US? DIDN'T **TRY**!

WE SUCCEEDED ...BUT THE LESS YOU KNOW ABOUT THAT, THE BETTER!

BUT WHEN DAWN CASTS A ROSY GLOW OVER THE SUNG MOUNTAIN...

ABBOT YUEH WANTS TO TALK TO THE FOREIGN DEVIL YOU TAKE HIM... I'M TO STAY HERE AND GUARD THE GIRL AND DOG...

SPLENDID! I'VE BEEN WAITING TO HAVE A CHAT!

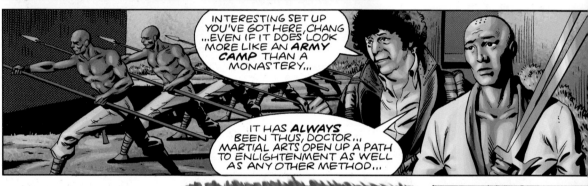

INTERESTING SET UP YOU'VE GOT HERE, CHANG ...EVEN IF IT DOES LOOK MORE LIKE AN **ARMY CAMP** THAN A MONASTERY...

IT HAS **ALWAYS** BEEN THUS, DOCTOR... MARTIAL ARTS OPEN UP A PATH TO ENLIGHTENMENT AS WELL AS ANY OTHER METHOD...

AND WHAT'S **THIS** PLACE WITH THE MASSIVE DOORS?

THAT? THE HALL OF THE **EIGHTEEN BRONZE MEN**...

WHERE OUR FIGHTING SKILLS ARE GIVEN THEIR **FINAL TESTING**...

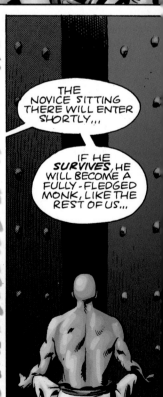

THE NOVICE SITTING THERE WILL ENTER SHORTLY...

IF HE **SURVIVES**, HE WILL BECOME A FULLY-FLEDGED MONK, LIKE THE REST OF US...

I SEE, ...TOUGH, IS IT?

YES, BUT I AM NOT PERMITTED TO SAY ANY MORE...

HE WILL NEED HIS WITS ABOUT HIM, THOUGH!

BUT THEN...

OH-OH! LI'S HERE!

SO I THINK IT'S TIME I WASN'T!

STOP HIM, CHANG! WOUND HIM IF YOU HAVE TO!

THIS IS YOUR BIG DAY, YOUNG WU! NO ONE WITHOUT FIVE YEARS TRAINING ENTERS HERE...AND THEN FEW HAVE THE COURAGE! THIS IS TRULY A PLACE WHERE THE WISE MAN FEARS TO TREAD...

SORRY! EXCUSE ME! IN A HURRY...

FOOLISH, I KNOW, BUT...

KE LANG!

HMM... AS SHARON WOULD SAY...

OH, BLIMEY!

NEXT: SECRET OF THE BRONZE MEN!

71

DOCTOR WHO

DRAGON'S CLAW

HELD PRISONER WITH SHARON IN THE SHAOLIN MONASTERY, THE DOCTOR HAS BROKEN FREE AND MADE HIS WAY INTO THE MYSTERIOUS HALL OF THE EIGHTEEN BRONZE MEN...

YOU'VE GOT THE *WRONG MAN*, CHAPS! I'M JUST A *TOURIST*!

HMM...*NOT LISTENING*, ARE YOU?

YAAAAA!

OOPS! *ALMOST CAUGHT ME ON THE HOP*!

ZAK!

PERHAPS THIS *WASN'T* SUCH A GOOD IDEA, AFTER ALL...

BUT THERE'S NO *GOING BACK* NOW!

GLANG!

MEANWHILE, OUTSIDE...

MASTER...HE'LL *DIE* IF WE LEAVE HIM IN THERE...!

SO BE IT...

SO BE IT? BUT WHAT HAS HE *DONE*?

MORE THAN *YOU* SEEM TO KNOW, BROTHER! LAST NIGHT HE SPOKE WITH *HSIANG THE ANCIENT*!

IMPOSSIBLE! I WAS WITH HIM FROM DUSK TO DAWN!

FOOL! I SAW HIM MYSELF!

WAPP!

COME ON...THERE MIGHT STILL BE ENOUGH LIFE IN HIM TO ANSWER A QUESTION OR TWO...

BUT...

PAST THE FIRST ROOM?

PERHAPS THIS FOREIGN DEVIL IS MORE DANGEROUS THAN I THOUGHT...

GO AND MAKE YOUR PEACE WITH CHANG... I DON'T WANT HIM GETTING SUSPICIOUS!

I'LL SEE WHERE THE CURLY-HAIRED ONE IS...

AND THEN I'LL SEE HIM DEAD!

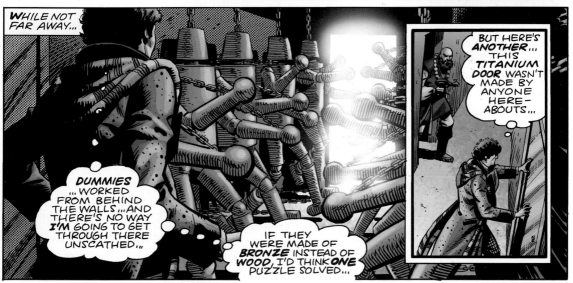

WHILE NOT FAR AWAY...

DUMMIES ...WORKED FROM BEHIND THE WALLS...AND THERE'S NO WAY I'M GOING TO GET THROUGH THERE UNSCATHED...

IF THEY WERE MADE OF BRONZE INSTEAD OF WOOD, I'D THINK ONE PUZZLE SOLVED...

BUT HERE'S ANOTHER... THIS TITANIUM DOOR WASN'T MADE BY ANYONE HERE-ABOUTS...

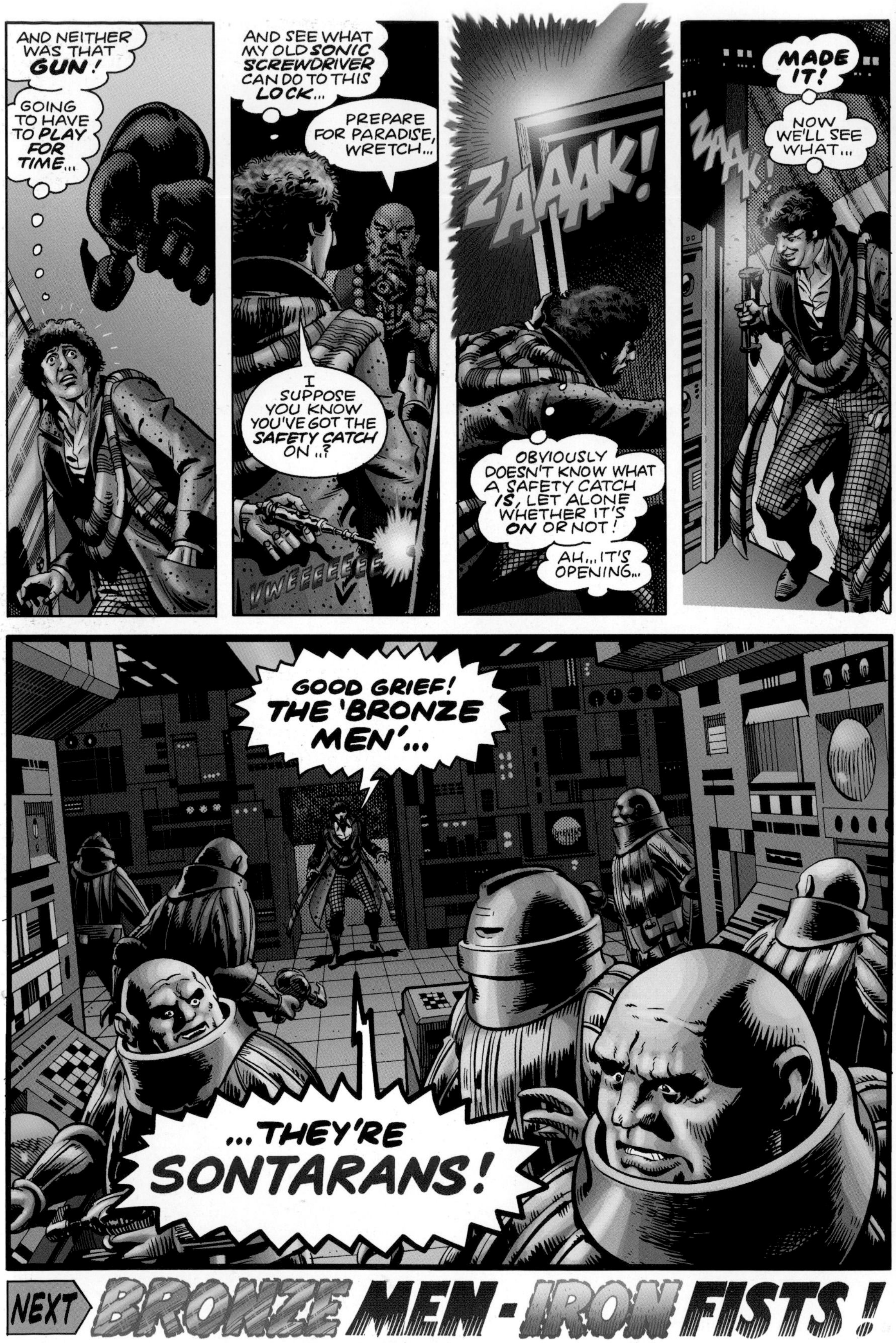
AND NEITHER WAS THAT GUN!
GOING TO HAVE TO PLAY FOR TIME...
AND SEE WHAT MY OLD SONIC SCREWDRIVER CAN DO TO THIS LOCK...
PREPARE FOR PARADISE, WRETCH...
I SUPPOSE YOU KNOW YOU'VE GOT THE SAFETY CATCH ON..?
VWEEEEEEE
ZAAAK!
OBVIOUSLY DOESN'T KNOW WHAT A SAFETY CATCH IS, LET ALONE WHETHER IT'S ON OR NOT!
AH... IT'S OPENING...
ZAAAK!
MADE IT!
NOW WE'LL SEE WHAT...
GOOD GRIEF! THE 'BRONZE MEN'...
...THEY'RE SONTARANS!
NEXT
BRONZE MEN - IRON FISTS!

DOCTOR WHO in.. DRAGON'S CLAW

Of the five holy peaks of China, MOUNT SUNG stands in the centre. Yet here, within the ancient SHAOLIN MONASTERY, lurks a band of the most UNHOLY beings in the universe...

To the monks, they are known as the EIGHTEEN BRONZE MEN...to the Doctor, as SONTARANS...

And now the battle lines are being drawn...

MEN OF BRONZE: FISTS OF IRON

WRITER= **STEVE MOORE** / ARTIST= **DAVE GIBBONS** / EDITOR= **PAUL NEARY**

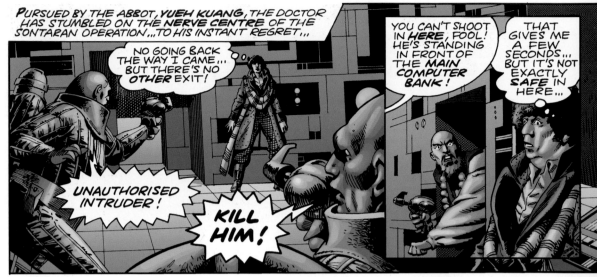

PURSUED BY THE ABBOT, *YUEH KUANG*, THE DOCTOR HAS STUMBLED ON THE *NERVE CENTRE* OF THE SONTARAN OPERATION...TO HIS INSTANT REGRET...

NO GOING BACK THE WAY I CAME... BUT THERE'S NO *OTHER* EXIT!

UNAUTHORISED INTRUDER!

KILL HIM!

YOU CAN'T SHOOT IN *HERE*, FOOL! HE'S STANDING IN FRONT OF THE *MAIN COMPUTER BANK*!

THAT GIVES ME A FEW SECONDS... BUT IT'S NOT EXACTLY *SAFE* IN HERE...

NOR, ALAS, OUTSIDE...

YOU MUST FORGIVE THE BLOW I STRUCK, BROTHER CHANG...

BUT THIS FOREIGN DEVIL *DOCTOR* IS SO GREAT A *THREAT*...

BUT ALL HE DID WAS CLIMB OVER THE WALL...

AND, TALKING OF WALLS...

NOW YOU CAN SHOOT HIM ...THERE'S NO EQUIP- MENT...

SOMETIMES I THINK I SHOULD CHANGE MY NAME FROM *DOCTOR* TO *DONALD*!

ZZAKK!

ALL I EVER SEEM TO DO IS *DUCK*!

UUNNNHH!

BROTHER LI! WHA..?

DOCTOR? WHAT ARE *YOU* DOING HERE?

RUNNING AWAY... COME ON!

BUT... RUNNING FROM *WHAT?*

ZZAKK!!!!

FROM *THAT!*

BAH! THEY'VE REACHED COVER! WE'VE GOT TO GET *AFTER* THEM...!

NO! YOU CAN'T LET THE NOVICES AND LAY-BROTHERS SEE YOU!

BUT DON'T WORRY... *NO ONE* FIGHTS THEIR WAY *INTO* OR *OUT OF* SHAOLIN!

AND THAT WOULD ALSO SEEM TO APPLY TO THE DOCTOR'S COMPANIONS, *SHARON* AND *K-9*, HELD PRISONER NEARBY...

WHAT'S GOING ON? THAT SOUNDED LIKE AN *EXPLOSION...*

STAY WHERE YOU ARE! IT'S NOTHING TO DO WITH *YOU!*

I THINK IT *IS*, BALDY...

STUN HIM, K-9!

COME ON, K-9—*HURRY UP!*

I CANNOT EXCEED THE SPEED LIMIT, MISTRESS.

SUPPOSE I'LL HAVE TO *CARRY YOU*, THEN...

AND SHORTLY...

DOCTOR! WHAT'S BEEN *HAPPENING?*

FAR TOO MUCH FOR MY *LIKING*, SHARON...

WE'VE GOT TO GET *MOVING* BEFORE THEY...

...SOUND THE ALARM!

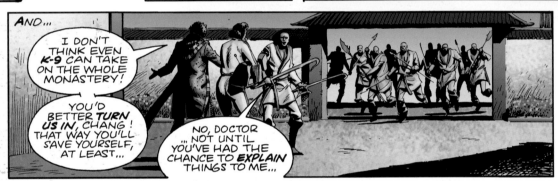

AND...

I DON'T THINK EVEN *K-9* CAN TAKE ON THE WHOLE MONASTERY!

YOU'D BETTER *TURN US IN*, CHANG! THAT WAY YOU'LL *SAVE* YOURSELF, AT LEAST...

NO, DOCTOR ...NOT UNTIL YOU'VE HAD THE CHANCE TO *EXPLAIN* THINGS TO ME...

YOU'LL *HELP* US, THEN?

YES...

BUT I CANNOT BRING MYSELF TO USE *WEAPONS* AGAINST MY BROTHERS...

BUT YOU CAN'T TAKE THEM ON *UNARMED*, CHANG...

THEY'LL *CUT YOU TO PIECES!*

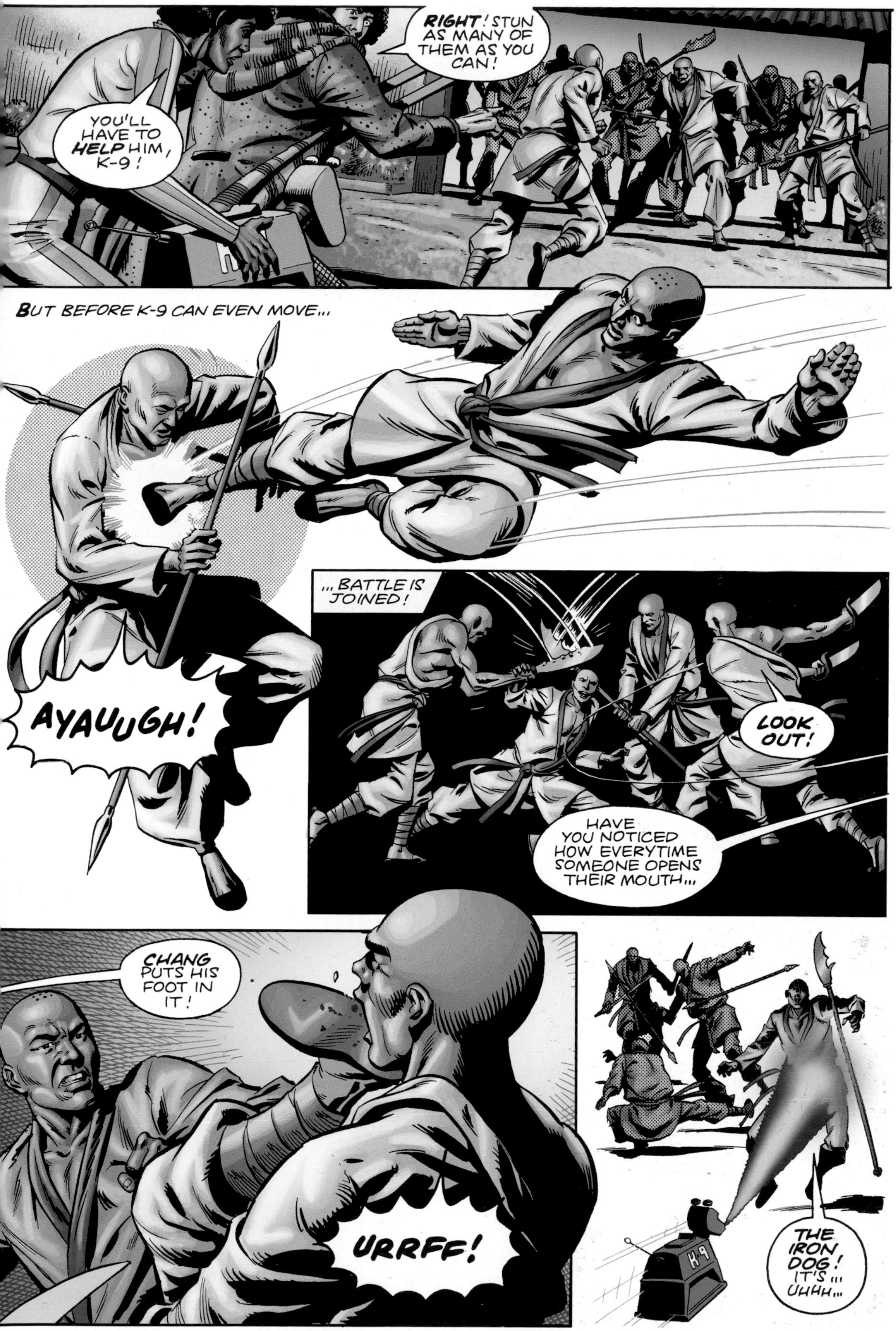
RIGHT! STUN AS MANY OF THEM AS YOU CAN!
YOU'LL HAVE TO HELP HIM, K-9!
BUT BEFORE K-9 CAN EVEN MOVE...
AYAUUGH!
...BATTLE IS JOINED!
LOOK OUT!
HAVE YOU NOTICED HOW EVERYTIME SOMEONE OPENS THEIR MOUTH...
CHANG PUTS HIS FOOT IN IT!
URRFF!
THE IRON DOG! IT'S... UHHH...

THEN...

MORE OF THEM, DOCTOR! IT'S HOPELESS!

HAVE TO THINK OF SOMETHING ELSE THEN...K-9!

HERE, BOY!

BE A GOOD DOG AND BLAST A...

HOLE IN THE WALL, MASTER...

BOOO...RRMME!!

ALMOST HUMAN, ISN'T HE?

AND, IN THE MOMENT OF SHOCKED SILENCE THAT FOLLOWS...

COME ON, CHANG! THAT'S MUCH TOO TIRING!

I'M GETTING TIRED JUST WATCHING!

SO LET'S HEAD FOR THE HILLS INSTEAD!

AND SOON, SAFE ON THE WOODED SLOPES OF MOUNT SUNG...

AND YOU SAY THE BRONZE MEN ARE ALIVE AND NOT OF THIS WORLD?

ARE THEY DEMONS, THEN?

YOU COULD CALL THEM THAT! THEY COME FROM A WORLD FAR AWAY FROM HERE...VERY FAR...

FOR CENTURIES THEY'VE BEEN FIGHTING A WAR AGAINST THEIR ARCH-ENEMIES, THE RUTANS...AND WILL BE STILL FOR CENTURIES YET...

I FIRST RAN INTO THEM ABOUT THREE HUNDRED YEARS AGO...YOUR TIME...

THREE HUNDRED YEARS AGO?!

THEY'RE SAVAGE...BRUTAL...THEY LIVE ONLY TO FIGHT...AND TO DIE A 'GLORIOUS' DEATH...

AND THEY'VE GOT THE **WEAPONS** TO KILL EVERYONE IN THE MONASTERY... YOU SAW THAT YOURSELF...

STRANGE...BUT IF AN **IMMORTAL** LIKE YOU SAYS SO, HOW CAN I FAIL TO BELIEVE...

I THOUGHT THEY WERE MECHANICAL **CONTRIVANCES**...LIKE YOUR IRON DOG...

BUT IF THEY'RE **ALIVE**, WHY DO THEY NEVER LEAVE THE BRONZE MEN HALL?

THAT'S WHAT **I'D** LIKE TO KNOW! WHAT **HAPPENS** IN THAT HALL, CHANG?

'I HAD SWORN NEVER TO SPEAK OF IT, BUT... ONCE PAST THE WOODEN DUMMIES, YOU MUST FACE THE **BRONZE MEN**...

'THEY PROVIDE THE **ULTIMATE TEST**, AND THEY ARE **UNIMAGINABLY SKILFUL**...ONLY THREE OR FIVE OUT OF TEN **SURVIVE**...

'TO PASS TO THE **FINAL CHAMBER**, WHERE THERE IS A **CAULDRON**...AND A **FIERCE LIGHT**...

AFTER LOOKING AT THAT, YOU REMEMBER **NOTHING**...UNTIL YOU ARE OUTSIDE AGAIN...

SOUNDS LIKE **HYPNOTISM**...THEY'RE PROBABLY IMPLANTING **POST-HYPNOTIC COMMANDS**...

POST-HYPNO-- HYP-- WHAT DOES **THAT** MEAN?

THAT'D **EXPLAIN** IT! WHY NORMALLY PEACEFUL MONKS...

HEAR ONE **KEY-WORD**...

AND START **KILLING EVERYONE IN SIGHT!**

81

CHINA, 1522 AD. SONTARAN INVADERS ARE HIDING IN THE SHAOLIN MONASTERY WHERE THEY ARE REVERED AS THE "EIGHTEEN BRONZEMEN"... AND USING HYPNOSIS TO TURN THE MONKS INTO KILLERS...

I DON'T *THINK* SO... BUT WE SET OFF FOR CHEKIANG ON THE ORDERS OF THE *EMPEROR*...

I STILL *CAN'T BELIEVE* OUR OWN *ABBOT* IS IN LEAGUE WITH *DEVILS*...

I'M SURE *HSIANG THE ANCIENT* COULD CONVINCE YOU OTHERWISE...

A *SINGLE WORD*... CAN *MAKE* ME KILL?

THAT'S *RIGHT*... DID ABBOT YUEH SAY ANYTHING *UNUSUAL* TO YOU BEFORE YOU FOUGHT THE *JAPANESE PIRATES?*

THINK I'LL HAVE ANOTHER WORD WITH THAT *FUNNY OLD FELLOW!* SHALL WE GO?

BUT THE DOCTOR AND HIS COMPANIONS ARE NOT THE ONLY ONES TRAVELLING ON *MOUNT SUNG* THIS DAY...

THIS SOLDIER... A MEMBER OF THE *PALACE GUARD*... HAS GALLOPED FOUR HORSES TO THE POINT OF COLLAPSE...

DOCTOR WHO
DRAGON'S CLAW

NOW, IN A SIMILAR STATE HIMSELF, HE BRINGS...

THE *WORD OF THE SON OF HEAVEN!* KNEEL... AS IF YOU WERE WITH- IN SIGHT OF THE *IMPERIAL ONE* HIM- SELF!

THIS MESSAGE DEMANDS THE PRESENCE OF *YUEH KUANG* -- THE DULY ORDAINED *ABBOT!*

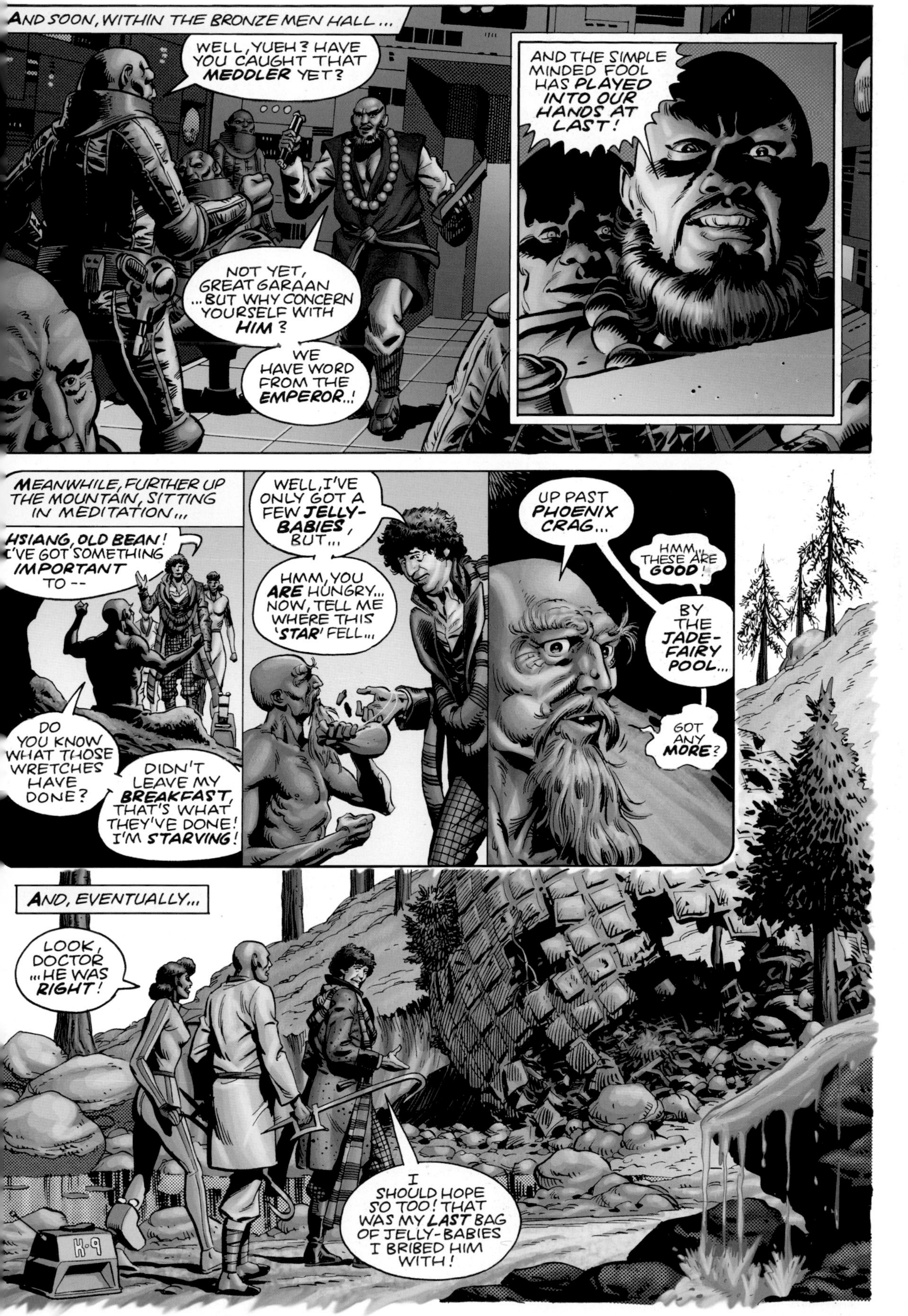
AND SOON, WITHIN THE BRONZE MEN HALL...
WELL, YUEH? HAVE YOU CAUGHT THAT MEDDLER YET?
NOT YET, GREAT GARAAN ...BUT WHY CONCERN YOURSELF WITH HIM?
WE HAVE WORD FROM THE EMPEROR..!
AND THE SIMPLE MINDED FOOL HAS PLAYED INTO OUR HANDS AT LAST!
MEANWHILE, FURTHER UP THE MOUNTAIN, SITTING IN MEDITATION...
HSIANG, OLD BEAN! I'VE GOT SOMETHING IMPORTANT TO --
DO YOU KNOW WHAT THOSE WRETCHES HAVE DONE?
DIDN'T LEAVE MY BREAKFAST, THAT'S WHAT THEY'VE DONE! I'M STARVING!
WELL, I'VE ONLY GOT A FEW JELLY-BABIES, BUT...
HMM, YOU ARE HUNGRY... NOW, TELL ME WHERE THIS 'STAR' FELL...
UP PAST PHOENIX CRAG...
HMM... THESE ARE GOOD!
BY THE JADE-FAIRY POOL...
GOT ANY MORE?
AND, EVENTUALLY...
LOOK, DOCTOR ...HE WAS RIGHT!
I SHOULD HOPE SO TOO! THAT WAS MY LAST BAG OF JELLY-BABIES I BRIBED HIM WITH!
K·9

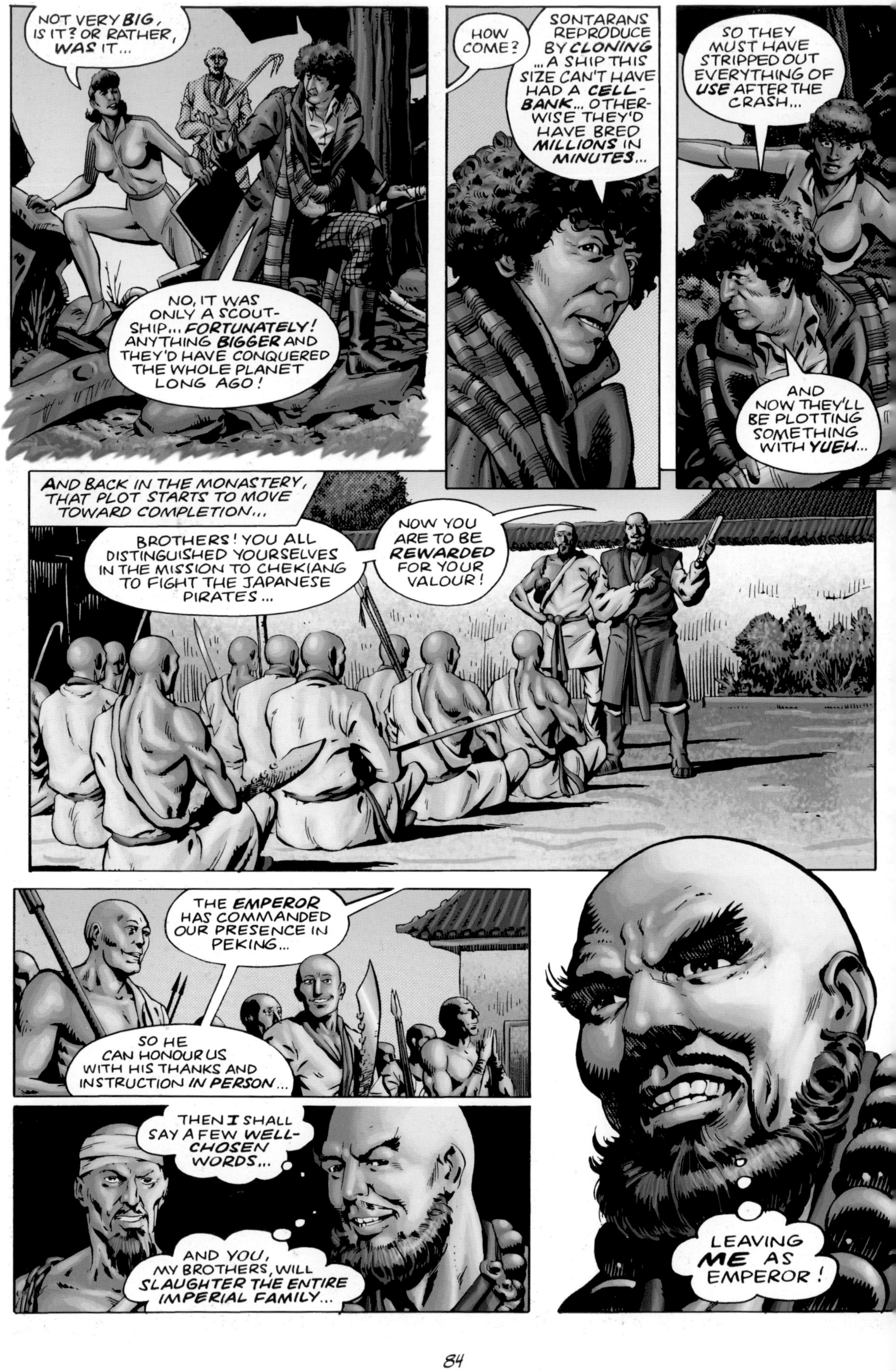

NOT VERY BIG, IS IT? OR RATHER, WAS IT...
NO, IT WAS ONLY A SCOUT-SHIP... FORTUNATELY! ANYTHING BIGGER AND THEY'D HAVE CONQUERED THE WHOLE PLANET LONG AGO!
HOW COME?
SONTARANS REPRODUCE BY CLONING ...A SHIP THIS SIZE CAN'T HAVE HAD A CELL-BANK... OTHER-WISE THEY'D HAVE BRED MILLIONS IN MINUTES...
SO THEY MUST HAVE STRIPPED OUT EVERYTHING OF USE AFTER THE CRASH...
AND NOW THEY'LL BE PLOTTING SOMETHING WITH YUEH...
AND BACK IN THE MONASTERY, THAT PLOT STARTS TO MOVE TOWARD COMPLETION...
BROTHERS! YOU ALL DISTINGUISHED YOURSELVES IN THE MISSION TO CHEKIANG TO FIGHT THE JAPANESE PIRATES...
NOW YOU ARE TO BE REWARDED FOR YOUR VALOUR!
THE EMPEROR HAS COMMANDED OUR PRESENCE IN PEKING...
SO HE CAN HONOUR US WITH HIS THANKS AND INSTRUCTION IN PERSON...
THEN I SHALL SAY A FEW WELL-CHOSEN WORDS...
AND YOU, MY BROTHERS, WILL SLAUGHTER THE ENTIRE IMPERIAL FAMILY...
LEAVING ME AS EMPEROR!

MEANWHILE...

I GUESS THIS MUST BE WHERE THEY HAD THEIR CONTROL PANELS...

BUT THIS LOOKS LIKE SOMEONE'S BROKEN JEWELLERY!

BE A GOOD DOG AND GIVE ME AN ANALYSIS OF THIS, K-9!

QUARTZ, MISTRESS. SILICON DIOXIDE IN PURE FORM... COMMONLY KNOWN AS ROCK CRYSTAL...

ROCK CRYSTAL? I HEAR THE ANNAMESE AMBASSADOR BROUGHT SUCH A THING AS TRIBUTE TO THE EMPEROR...

A CRYSTAL AS BIG AS A MAN'S FIST...

SCAN OF CRYSTAL LATTICES SHOWS IT WAS USED FOR AMPLIFYING HYPER-SPACE RADIO EMISSION...

SO THAT'S WHAT THE SONTARANS ARE AFTER!

WITH THEIR OWN SMASHED THEY NEED THE EMPEROR'S CRYSTAL TO RIG UP A TRANSMITTER POWERFUL ENOUGH TO CONTACT THEIR OWN FORCES!

BUT TO GET THAT, THEY'D HAVE TO KILL THE EMPEROR!

DOES THAT SURPRISE YOU?

HOLD ON! THERE'S SOMEONE OVER THERE...

THE WATER-CARRIER... IT'S AH YING... ONLY ONE OF OUR NOVICES, BUT A FRIEND...

I'LL GO AND SPEAK TO HIM...

THE SONTARANS MUST HAVE OFFERED *YUEH* THE *THRONE*, WHILE *THEY* GO FOR THE *CRYSTAL*...

BUT OUR ABBOT ISN'T GOING TO *SIT ON IT LONG* WHEN THE *INVASION FORCE* ARRIVES!

THEN...

EVIL NEWS! YUEH'S ABOUT TO TAKE A PICKED GROUP OF MONKS TO *PEKING!* ALL THE ONES WHO FOUGHT THE PIRATES!

HMM... YOU TWO HAD BETTER SLIP BACK INTO THE MONASTERY...

SABOTAGE SOMETHING... STIR UP *TROUBLE*... *ANYTHING* TO DELAY THEM!

AND *SHARON* AND I'LL JOIN YOU AS SOON AS WE CAN...!

AND SOON THEREAFTER...

WE'LL SAY *SORRY* WHEN YOU WAKE UP, BROTHER KUNG...

UUNNH...

NOW... GATHER AS MANY NOVICES AS YOU CAN... I'LL MEET YOU IN THE MAIN COURTYARD...

AND...

THE *'BRONZE MEN'* ARE *DEVILS* FROM ANOTHER WORLD... AND ABBOT YUEH'S *PLOTTING* WITH THEM!

THE *IMMORTAL* WITH THE IRON DOG TOLD ME THIS!

WHAT'S HAPPENING HERE?

CHANG!

WE *DEMAND* TO LOOK INSIDE THE *BRONZE MEN* HALL! SHOW US WHAT'S GOING ON!

FOOLS! ONLY THE *ABBOT* CAN GIVE PERMISSION FOR THAT!

AND *THAT'S* WHO WE'VE GOT HERE! *HSIANG THE ANCIENT*...THE *REAL* ABBOT!

WHERE'S MY BREAKFAST?

BE A GOOD CHAP, HSIANG! SAY WHAT I TOLD YOU ... AND *THEN* WE'LL GET YOU SOMETHING TO EAT!

WHAT? OH, YES ..!

AS THE ORIGINALLY ORDAINED ABBOT ...DEPOSED BY TREACHERY... I ORDER THE OPENING OF THE BRONZE MEN HALL!

WAS THAT ALRIGHT? I'M HUNGRY...

OPEN THE HALL!

CAN'T STOP THEM ON MY *OWN*! *YUEH* WILL HAVE TO HANDLE THIS!

AND MOMENTS LATER...

STOP ALL THIS FOOLISHNESS, CHANG! YOU CAN'T DEFY *ME*!

WE *CAN*...

AND WE *DO*!

AH, BUT ALL I HAVE TO DO IS *SAY THE WORD* ...AND YOU WILL BECOME ANOTHER ONE OF MY *KILLING SLAVES*!

AND YOU CAN'T *REACH* ME IN TIME TO STOP ME SAYING IT!

MUMBLE YOUR SPELL, FALSE PRIEST! WE WILL *NEVER* GIVE UP!

GET READY TO *RECORD* THIS, K-9!

THE BRONZE BUDDHA HAS A HEART OF IRON!

THAT'LL FIX HIM!

WHAT?!

SORRY... DON'T THINK HE HEARD YOU...

CURSE THE FOREIGN DEVIL! I CAN'T SAY IT AGAIN OR THE OTHERS WILL SNAP OUT OF THEIR TRANCES!

BUT THEY'LL BE MORE THAN ENOUGH TO TAKE CARE OF CHANG!

AND WITHIN MOMENTS...

KILL THEM! THEY'RE YOUR ENEMIES... KILL THEM!

TIME TO PLAY BACK, K-9!

THE BRONZE BUDDHA HAS A HEART OF IRON!

WHAT... AH YING?

WHAT AM I DOING?

WHY ARE WE FIGHTING OUR OWN BROTHERS?

BECAUSE YUEH FORCED YOU TO... BUT NO MORE!

OOPS! I FORGOT YOU, CHANG... WHEN WE SWITCHED THE OTHERS **OFF**, WE SWITCHED YOU **ON**!

ER...YOU'RE NOT GOING TO DO ANYTHING **RASH**, ARE YOU?

STAND ASIDE, DOCTOR... I **KNOW** MY ENEMIES NOW!

YUEH KUANG AND LI SAN... YOU'VE MADE ME WHAT I **AM**...NOW YOU'LL **PAY**!

LI CAN KEEP CHANG OCCUPIED...WHILE I DISPOSE OF **HSIANG THE ANCIENT** AND THAT INFERNAL **DOCTOR**...!

BUT...

K-9!

TAKEN CARE OF, MASTER!

WHA...?

AND BEFORE K-9 CAN FIRE AGAIN...

BAH! STAR-WEAPON OR NOT... I CAN STILL MANGLE AN **OLD FOOL** LIKE YOU!

OLD? FOOL?

HRUMPH! YOUNG WHIPPER-SNAPPER!

GLARG!

89

DOCTOR! HERE COMES CHANG!

ARE YOU ALRIGHT, CHANG? WHAT ABOUT LI?

LI FOUGHT WELL...

I'LL HAVE TO GET HIM AWAY WHERE NO ONE ELSE CAN HEAR AND PLAY BACK K-9'S TAPE...OTHERWISE HE'LL CREATE HAVOC!

BUT THERE'S NO TIME FOR THAT NOW! WE'VE GOT TO GET INTO THE BRONZE MEN HALL!

AND...

FULL-POWER BLAST THAT WALL, K-9...AND WE'LL SEE WHAT SORT OF HORNET'S NEST THAT STIRS UP!

AFFIRMATIVE, MASTER!

VA-WUMMPF!

NOW, AS SOON AS ANY SONTARANS APPEAR, I WANT YOU TO STOP THEM, K-9...

MASTER...!

ZZZ ZAKK!

YAUUGH!

NO NEED FOR YOUR IRON DOG, DOCTOR...

THEY WILL NOT BE COMING OUT!

NO, CHANG! YOU CAN'T...!

YOORGH!

AYGAAH!

CAN YOU...?

AND THEN, AFTER WHAT SEEMS AN ETERNITY OF SILENCE...

IT IS...

...OVER.

BROTHER CHANG!

MOMENTS LATER...

ALL DEAD?

YES... BUT WHAT ABOUT CHANG?

HE MAY RECOVER... IT IS IN THE HANDS OF THE BUDDHA...

AND, WITHIN THE HOUR, A STRANGE CALM FALLS OVER THE ANCIENT MONASTERY ...A RETURN TO PSEUDO-NORMALITY...

WELL, OLD HSIANG...LOOKS LIKE YOU'LL BE REINSTATED AS ABBOT NOW...

RIGHT! FIRST THING TO DO IS ORDER A FEAST...ALL THE FOOD I CAN EAT...

YOU CAN HAVE SOME TOO, OF COURSE...

BUT NOT MUCH...

AH, NO ...WE'LL HAVE TO BE GOING... IT'S A LONG RIDE BACK TO THE TARDIS...

IF I'M EVER PASSING THIS TIME AGAIN, I DROP OFF A BAG OF JELLY-BABIES FOR YOU...

THE END.

NEXT ISSUE THE DOCTOR, SHARON AND K-9 MEET...THE COLLECTOR!

NWORPVWORP

THE COLLECTOR

BY JOVE! I DO BELIEVE I'VE GOT IT!

BLACKCASTLE RO

WRITER= **STEVE MOORE** / ARTIST= **DAVE GIBBONS** / EDITOR= **PAUL NEARY**

IN SPITE OF THE **RANDOMISER** IN THE CONTROLS, I'VE ACTUALLY GOT YOU **HOME**, SHARON!

TWENTIETH CENTURY **BLACKCASTLE**, ENGLAND, EARTH!

REALLY, DOCTOR...?

ONLY TROUBLE IS, I'M NOT SURE I **WANT** TO GO HOME NOW...NOT NOW I'VE **GROWN UP**!

OH, OF COURSE YOU DO! 'NO PLACE LIKE HOME'!

WHY, I EVEN LIKE **GALLIFREY** ...SOMETIMES...

BUT, JUST AS THEY ARE ABOUT TO STEP OUTSIDE...

BLIMEY, DOCTOR... **LOOK OUT**!

WHAT'S **THAT**?

I'D GUESS WE'VE BEEN PICKED UP BY A **TELEPORT-BEAM** ...AND IT'S TAKEN THE **WHOLE TARDIS** WITH IT...

SEEMS HARD TO BELIEVE, I KNOW, BUT...

AND THEN THE TARDIS MAKES ITS SECOND MATERIALISATION IN A MATTER OF MINUTES...

I THINK SOMEONE WANTS TO HAVE A WORD WITH US...

SO **NOW** WHERE ARE WE, DOCTOR?

AS FAR AS I CAN TELL FROM THIS, WE SEEM TO BE IN THE **ASTEROID BELT**...

BUT IT APPEARS THERE'S A BREATHABLE ATMOSPHERE OUTSIDE...

BUT WHEN THEY EMERGE...

HMM...A COMPLETELY EMPTY ROOM! NO SIGN OF A **TELEPORT-MACHINE** IN HERE...BUT IT CAN'T BE FAR AWAY!

THESE DOORS ARE **LOCKED**, DOCTOR!

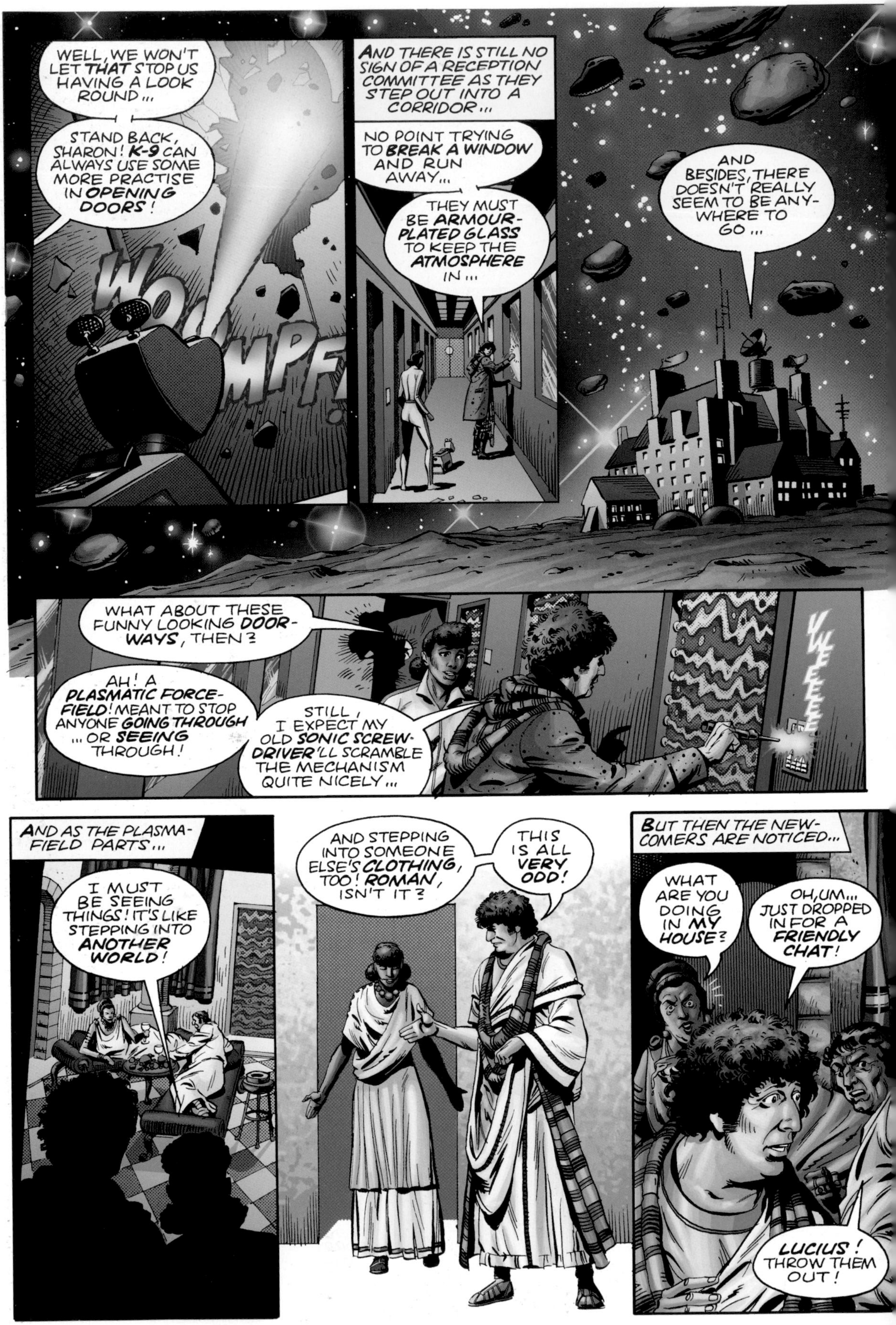

WELL, WE WON'T LET THAT STOP US HAVING A LOOK ROUND...
STAND BACK, SHARON! K-9 CAN ALWAYS USE SOME MORE PRACTISE IN OPENING DOORS!
WOOMPF!
AND THERE IS STILL NO SIGN OF A RECEPTION COMMITTEE AS THEY STEP OUT INTO A CORRIDOR...
NO POINT TRYING TO BREAK A WINDOW AND RUN AWAY...
THEY MUST BE ARMOUR-PLATED GLASS TO KEEP THE ATMOSPHERE IN...
AND BESIDES, THERE DOESN'T REALLY SEEM TO BE ANYWHERE TO GO...
WHAT ABOUT THESE FUNNY LOOKING DOORWAYS, THEN?
AH! A PLASMATIC FORCE-FIELD! MEANT TO STOP ANYONE GOING THROUGH ...OR SEEING THROUGH!
STILL, I EXPECT MY OLD SONIC SCREWDRIVER'LL SCRAMBLE THE MECHANISM QUITE NICELY...
VWEEEEE
AND AS THE PLASMA-FIELD PARTS...
I MUST BE SEEING THINGS! IT'S LIKE STEPPING INTO ANOTHER WORLD!
AND STEPPING INTO SOMEONE ELSE'S CLOTHING, TOO! ROMAN, ISN'T IT?
THIS IS ALL VERY ODD!
BUT THEN THE NEWCOMERS ARE NOTICED...
WHAT ARE YOU DOING IN MY HOUSE?
OH, UM... JUST DROPPED IN FOR A FRIENDLY CHAT!
LUCIUS! THROW THEM OUT!

BUT MAYBE WE CAN TALK *ANOTHER* DAY...!

YOU *CALLED*, SIR..?

ER... BYE!

AND THAT'S *ANOTHER* ODD THING! WE'VE BOTH BEEN TALKING *FLUENT LATIN* FOR THE LAST COUPLE OF MINUTES...I ONLY JUST REALISED...

IT'S AS IF WE'D STEPPED INTO A *FROZEN MOMENT* OF TIME ...WHERE EVERYTHING'S *EXACTLY* AS IT WAS THEN...

BLIMEY! LOOK AT US NOW!

THAT'S THE TROUBLE... EVERYONE'S *LOOKING* AT US!

*EXCUSE US....*JUST *PASSING* THROUGH!

AND AT LAST...

PHEW! BACK IN THE CORRIDOR AGAIN! HELLO, K-9!

WHAT DO YOU THINK YOU'RE *UP TO?*

I BROUGHT YOU HERE FOR MY *TWENTIETH* CENTURY ROOM... NOT TO CREATE HAVOC IN THE *THIRD* AND *EIGHTEENTH!*

AND WHAT DO YOU THINK *YOU'RE* UP TO? KIDNAPPING PEOPLE BY *TELEPORT-BEAM* AND KEEPING THEM IN *TIME-STASIS CAPSULES*?

HMM...THIS IS STRANGE! I DIDN'T THINK YOU EARTH-PEOPLE HAD SUCH *ADVANCED* KNOWLEDGE

NONE OF MY *OTHER* SPECIMENS DO!

PROBABLY BECAUSE NONE OF YOUR OTHER 'SPECIMENS' ARE *TIME–LORDS* FROM GALLIFREY!

ACCORDING TO THIS SCANNER, YOU'VE GOT *TWO HEART-BEATS!*

OH DEAR! I KNEW SHE'D MAKE A *MISTAKE* SOONER OR LATER!

FUNNY THAT... I DIDN'T THINK EARTH *HAD* MANY OFF-PLANET VISITORS!

WELL, I'LL GET HER TO *SEND YOU BACK!* SORRY YOU'VE BEEN TROUBLED!

JUST LIKE *THAT*? I THINK WE DESERVE AN EXPLANATION, AT LEAST!

YES, I SUPPOSE YOU *DO*! I'M *VARAN TAK*, FROM THE ANTHROPOLOGY UNIT ON *OSKERION*...

I WAS GOING TO EARTH TO STUDY THE DEVELOPING CIVILISATION THERE...WHEN WAS IT? ABOUT TWO THOUSAND YEARS AGO...! WE WERE *THIS* CLOSE WHEN A ROGUE ASTEROID KNOCKED OUT THE *DRIVE-UNIT*...AND MOST OF THE *COMMUNICATIONS*, TOO...

"PROBABLY STILL BE ANOTHER *HUNDRED YEARS* BEFORE OUR DISTRESS CALL'S PICKED UP! I'LL BE *MIDDLE-AGED* BY THEN!"

SHE MANAGED TO PUT US DOWN HERE...AND SHE'S BUILT ALL THIS TO KEEP ME ALIVE AND COMFORTABLE...

ALONG WITH THE SHORT-RANGE TELEPORT TERMINAL... *USEFUL* THAT...

THAT'S HOW I PICK UP SPECIMENS FOR MY *ANTHROPOLOGICAL* COLLECTION...OH, MAYBE IT'S *WRONG* TO KIDNAP THEM...BUT STUDY KEEPS ME *SANE*...

PER-HAPS! BUT WHO'S THIS '*SHE*'?

WHY...THE *SHIP HERSELF*! EXCEPT SHE'S REBUILT HERSELF INTO THIS *HOUSE* NOW...

BUT THE ENTIRE STRUCTURE'S A *CONSCIOUS INTELLIGENT* COMPUTER, WHOSE FUNCTIONS ARE TO PROTECT AND SUSTAIN *ME*...

WITH FEMINISED VOCAL AND BEHAVIOURAL PATTERNS...

LITERALLY... A '*MOTHER*' SHIP...

MORE OF A *COMPANION* REALLY...BUT THOUGH SHE'S *ALL AROUND* US...

THE MAIN BRAIN-UNIT HAS BEEN *HUMANISED* EVEN MORE...

BUT WHY DON'T YOU JUST TELEPORT TO EARTH YOURSELF?

HOW I WISH I COULD! SHE'LL AGREE TO SEND YOU BACK...

BUT FOR SOME REASON SHE REFUSES TO LET ME LEAVE!

WELL, MAYBE WE SHOULD HAVE A LOOK AT THIS TELEPORT TERMINAL OF YOURS...

AND IF I ARRANGED TO GET YOU TO EARTH ...WOULD YOU STOP KIDNAPPING PEOPLE? FOR GOOD..?

IF YOU COULD...THEN YES, I SUPPOSE I WOULD...

BUT... SEE! I CAN'T GET NEAR IT... THAT COMES ON AUTOMATICALLY EVERY TIME I APPROACH!

HMM...NASTY LITTLE ELECTRIC ARC PROJECTOR UP THERE...BIT TOO COMPLICATED FOR THE SONIC SCREW-DRIVER...

THIS IS A JOB FOR YOU, K-9 ...PINPOINT BLASTING!

SZZK

ALRIGHT, VARAN TAK, THAT SHOULD HAVE CLEARED UP THE PROBLEM...SO THAT'S OUR SIDE OF THE BAR-GAIN.

MAKE SURE YOU KEEP YOURS!

I WILL ...AND I'LL ALWAYS BE GRATEFUL!

WELL, THAT SEEMS TO WRAP THAT UP, SHARON!

WASN'T SUCH A BAD SORT, AFTER ALL ...

SO LET'S GET BACK TO THE TARDIS BEFORE ...OOPS!

WHAT... HAVE YOU DONE?

K-9... SWITCH TO ELECTRONIC SCRAMBLE...

OH, NO!

K-9!

POOR OLD **K-9**! WHAT WILL I DO **WITHOUT** YOU?

DOCTOR... THE ROBOT...

FOOLS! ALL OF YOU ...AND **VARAN TAK** MOST OF ALL!

BUT AS THE TELEPORT GLOWS INTO REVERSE...

TOO LATE! I **TRIED** TO PROTECT YOU, VARAN TAK ... FOR YOU WERE FULL OF **NATURAL LIFE**...

AND NOW YOU ARE ...**SO DEAD**...

DEAD? OH DEAR... **THAT** WASN'T SUPPOSED TO HAPPEN...

POISONED...HE HAD NO RESISTANCE TO THE **INDUSTRIAL POLLUTION**...IN YOUR EARTH'S AIR...

THAT'S WHY ... IN RECENT CENTURIES...I WOULD NOT **LET** HIM GO!

SHE SEEMS QUITE UPSET, DOCTOR...FOR A **ROBOT**...

AND WHY **NOT**? I HAVE... **CHERISHED** HIM FOR **TWENTY CENTURIES**... AND NOW...

EVEN A **ROBOT** CAN FEEL ... **LONELY**...

BUT THEN...

THE INSTRUMENT READINGS WHEN WE LANDED **WERE** ODD... PERHAPS THERE'S A WAY OUT OF THIS...

BUT IT WOULD MEAN NO MORE **TELEPORT-KIDNAPPINGS** TO KEEP VARAN TAK HAPPY...!

I DO NOT...UNDER-STAND...BUT IF YOU CAN **RESTORE HIM** TO LIFE!

ANOTHER MINUTE FINDS THE THREE WHO REMAIN INSIDE THE TARDIS...

I'M HOPING THE **RANDOMISER** WON'T COME INTO PLAY...AS WE'RE NOT ACTUALLY **GOING ANYWHERE**...

BUT I THINK WE CAN UTILISE THE TIME-STASIS FIELDS AROUND US TO DO SOMETHING **RATHER CLEVER**...

AND WHEN THE TARDIS'S MIGHTY ENGINES AGAIN FADE INTO SILENCE...

WE ARE... STILL IN THE SAME PLACE! HOW CAN **THIS** HELP?

SAME PLACE... **DIFFERENT TIME**... I **THINK**! COME ON...

AND HOPE I'VE GOT THIS **RIGHT**!

RIGHT INDEED, FOR THEY HAVE HOPPED BACK HERE MINUTES, TO...

HMM... NASTY LITTLE *ELECTRIC ARC PROJECTOR* UP THERE... BIT TOO COMPLICATED FOR...

ONLY ONE WAY QUICK ENOUGH TO STOP THIS... I'M GOING TO HAVE TO...

SOCK MYSELF ON THE JAW!

WOK!

OOF!

NOW, K-9... *BLAST THE TELEPORT DEVICE!* COMPLETE DESTRUCTION!

NO!

AND THE ROOM REELS WITH A BLINDING, EXPLOSIVE FLASH...

BA·VOOMPF!

YET, WHEN THE SMOKE CLEARS...

DOCTOR...OUR *DUPLICATE SELVES*... THEY'VE *DISAPPEARED!*

RIGHT! WHEN I *DESTROYED* THE TELEPORT, *THAT WHOLE FUTURE* IN WHICH I SENT VARAN TAK TO EARTH WENT *OUT OF EXISTENCE* ...ALONG WITH OUR DUPLICATES...

AND THAT MEANS K-9 *DIDN'T* GET BLOWN UP...

AND VARAN TAK'S *STILL ALIVE*, TOO!

STILL ALIVE? DID SOMETHING *HAPPEN* TO ME?

WELL, I'M SURE *SHE'LL* HAVE PLENTY OF TIME TO TELL YOU WHILE YOU'RE WAITING TO BE PICKED UP! AFTER ALL, *SHE* SAW IT HAPPEN...

AND NOW I THINK WE'LL GET BACK TO THE TARDIS ...BEFORE ANYTHING ELSE HAPPENS TO *US!*

THE END.

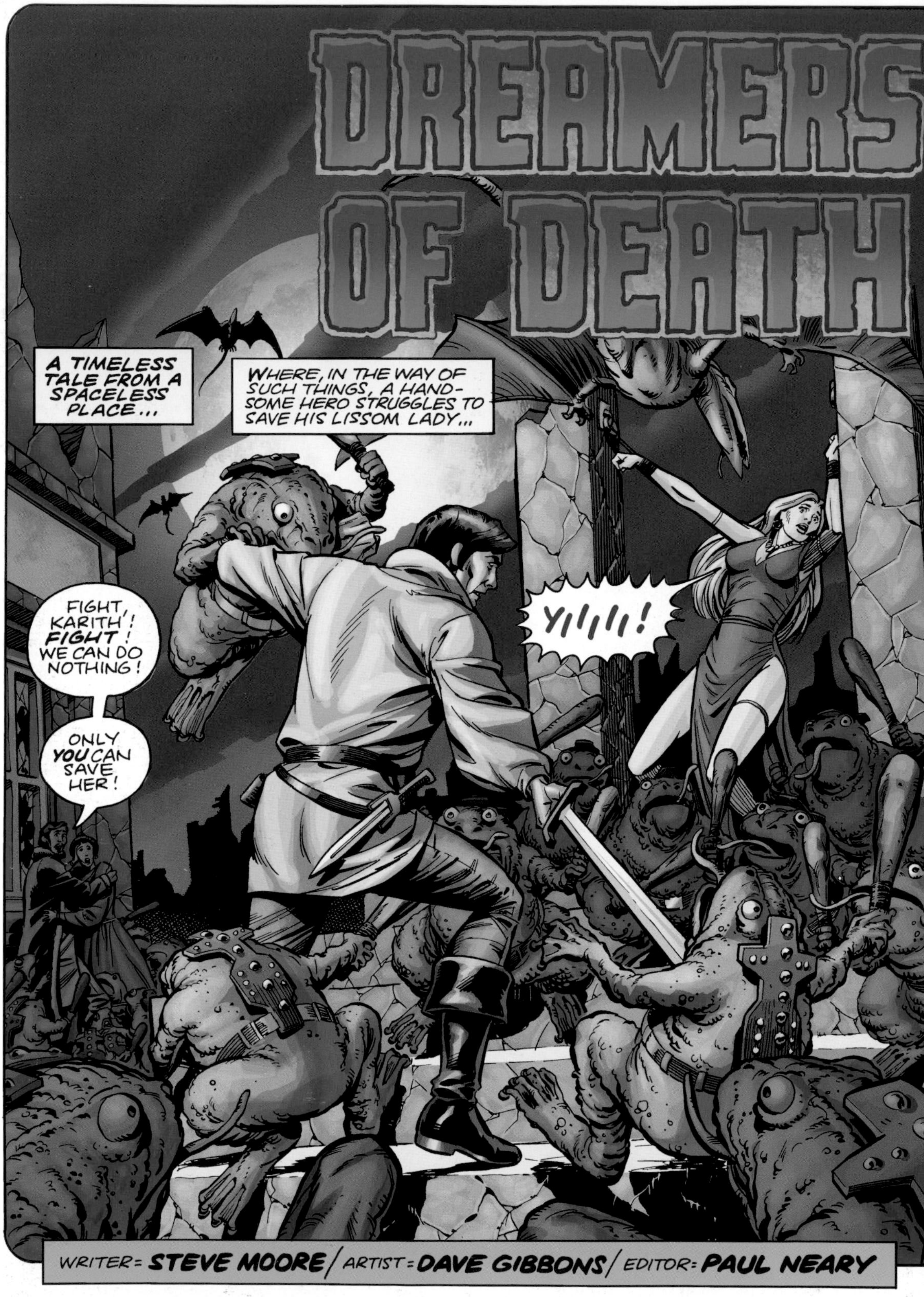
DREAMERS OF DEATH
A TIMELESS TALE FROM A SPACELESS PLACE...
WHERE, IN THE WAY OF SUCH THINGS, A HANDSOME HERO STRUGGLES TO SAVE HIS LISSOM LADY...
FIGHT, KARITH! FIGHT! WE CAN DO NOTHING!
ONLY YOU CAN SAVE HER!
YIIIII!
WRITER= STEVE MOORE / ARTIST= DAVE GIBBONS / EDITOR= PAUL NEARY

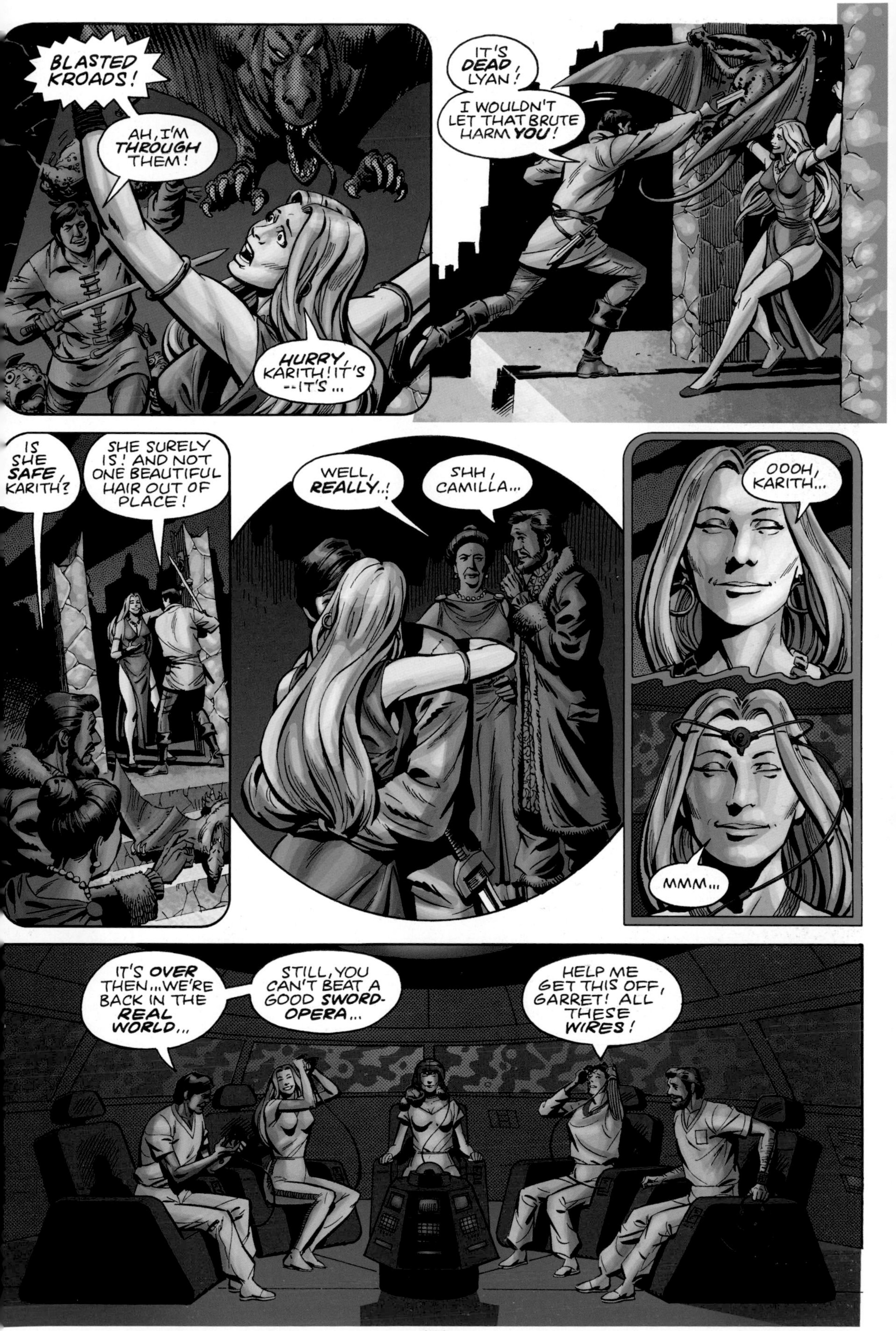
BLASTED KROADS!
AH, I'M THROUGH THEM!
HURRY, KARITH! IT'S --IT'S...
IT'S DEAD, LYAN!
I WOULDN'T LET THAT BRUTE HARM YOU!
IS SHE SAFE, KARITH?
SHE SURELY IS! AND NOT ONE BEAUTIFUL HAIR OUT OF PLACE!
WELL, REALLY..!
SHH, CAMILLA...
OOOH, KARITH...
MMM...
IT'S OVER THEN... WE'RE BACK IN THE REAL WORLD...
STILL, YOU CAN'T BEAT A GOOD SWORD-OPERA...
HELP ME GET THIS OFF, GARRET! ALL THESE WIRES!

I HOPE YOU ENJOYED YOUR DREAM, EVERY-ONE!

YES, INDEED! YOU DREAM A GOOD STORY, SCYLLA!

ACTION, HUMOUR, ROMANCE ...IT WAS EXCELLENT!

AH, WELL, I HAD AN EXCELLENT CAST ...IT MAKES THINGS SO MUCH EASIER...

YOU MAKE A DASHING HERO, KARITH...

AND YOU, LYAN, A CHARMING AND BEAUTIFUL HEROINE! A GOOD MATCH FOR HIM...

TOO RIGHT!

HA! I HAVEN'T SEEN MY DAUGHTER BLUSH LIKE THAT FOR AGES! GO ON, KARITH, SHE'S PROBABLY HEADING FOR THE GARDEN...

NOW, SCYLLA, ABOUT YOUR BILL...

'DREAMS DELUXE' WILL INVOICE YOU AS USUAL, MR BERRACE ...BUT NOW I MUST GET ON TO MY NEXT CLIENT...

IT'S BEEN A PLEASURE DREAMING FOR YOU! GOODBYE...

AND SCYLLA, LIVING AND WORKING IN A WORLD OF DREAMS, HARDLY NOTICES AN UNUSUAL ARRIVAL IN THE REAL WORLD...

AS THE TARDIS PUTS IN AN UNSCHEDULED APPEARANCE...

BY JOVE! IT'S UNICEPTER IV! THAT'S A BIT OF LUCK... I'VE GOT OLD FRIENDS HERE!

OF COURSE, THEY MIGHT BE YOUNG FRIENDS ...DEPENDS WHEN WE'VE ARRIVED!

IT'S A **FARMING WORLD**...MOST OF THE PEOPLE LIVE HERE IN THIS ONE CITY...WHILE ROBOTS DO THE PLANTING AND REAPING...

HMM...THAT'S **ODD**...

I'D **S'WEAR** THAT WOMAN'S FUR **GROWLED** AT ME!

YOU MUST BE **HEARING THINGS**, DOCTOR! COME ON, WHERE ARE YOUR FRIENDS?

AND, SOON ENOUGH...

GARRET BERRACE AND HIS WIFE, **CAMILLA**! AH, AND WHERE'S THAT LITTLE MINX, **LYAN**?

LITTLE? COME ON, DOCTOR, I'VE GOT A SURPRISE FOR YOU...

AHEM!

DOCTOR! I HAVEN'T SEEN YOU FOR...WHAT IS IT, SIX OR SEVEN YEARS?

AND THIS IS **KARITH** ...THEY'RE TO BE MARRIED AT THE NEXT TWO-MOON FESTIVAL...

WELL, **HOW TIME FLIES**...AS THEY SAY IN MY LINE OF WORK...

WE'VE BEEN HAVING A LOVELY DREAM, DOCTOR!

WHAT, **BOTH** OF YOU?

NO, **ALL** OF US!

WITH A **PROFESSIONAL DREAMER**! IT STARTED THREE YEARS AGO...AND REPLACED TELEVISION IN NO TIME AT ALL...

ONE OF THE NATIVE ANIMALS, THE **SLINTH**, WAS FOUND TO HAVE **TELEPATHIC POWERS**...AND THEY CAN LIVE IN PERFECT UNION WITH HUMANS!

BERRACE LEADS THE DOCTOR INTO HIS HOUSE'S **DREAM-ROOM**...

THESE HEAD-PIECES CONNECT US TO THE DREAMER...AND WITH THE AID OF THE **SLINTH**...WE ALL TAKE PART IN A **FULLY-CONTROLLED DREAM-STORY**...ON WHATEVER SUBJECT WE CHOOSE...

SOME **RICH** PEOPLE, LIKE **LORD VEITH**, HAVE **PERSONAL DREAMERS** ON THEIR PERMANENT STAFF...

OH, DADDY... WE'VE **GOT** TO GET A DREAMER WHILE THE DOCTOR'S HERE! IT'S THE **COMPLETE FRENZY**, AFTER ALL!

COMPLETE FRENZY? OH...YOU MEAN IT'S **ALL THE RAGE**!

WELL, AS LONG AS IT'S NOTHING **TOO EXCITING**! YOU KNOW WHAT AN **UNADVENTUROUS SORT** I AM, GARRET...

I'LL SEE IF I CAN HIRE **VERNOR ALLEN**...HIS **DREAMSCAPES** ARE TRULY **POETIC**...

AS THE DAY FADES SLOWLY INTO NIGHT...

YOU KNOW, DOCTOR, I ALWAYS THOUGHT OF YOU AS A **LONER**...IT'S A BIT **STRANGE** TO SEE YOU JUST RELAXING WITH FRIENDS...

WELL, NO ONE SPENDS **ALL** THEIR TIME FIXING UP THE UNIVERSE, SHARON...

EXCUSE ME, DOCTOR...

I DON'T WANT TO **WORRY** YOU, DOCTOR, BUT I JUST HEARD THERE'S BEEN AN **ACCIDENT**! LORD VEITH, HIS DREAMER, AND TWO OTHERS HAVE BEEN KILLED...

THEY THINK IT WAS AN **ELECTRICAL FAULT**, BUT THEY'RE STILL WORKING THERE...

IT'S NEVER HAPPENED BEFORE, SO IT'S PROBABLY JUST ONE OF THOSE THINGS! STILL, I'LL CHECK ALL MY APPARATUS...

RIGHT...AND I THINK I'LL HAVE A QUICK WORD WITH K-9...

AND NOT LONG AFTER THE CHECKS HAVE BEEN MADE

GOOD EVENING, EVERYONE... I'M **VERNOR ALLEN**, YOUR DREAMER FOR TONIGHT...

AND I SEE WE'VE GOT OFF-WORLD **VISITORS**, TOO! THIS IS VERY PLEASANT...

SO THIS IS YOUR **SLINTH**, VERNOR? ER...IS HE SAFE TO TOUCH?

OF COURSE! A SLINTH IS A DREAMER'S BEST FRIEND! HIS NAME'S **MIKI**...

HASN'T LEFT MY SHOULDER FOR NEARLY THREE YEARS...

AND ARE **YOU** GOING TO BE IN THIS DREAM, VERNOR?

I'M AFRAID NOT...THE DREAMER'S TOO BUSY CONTROLLING THINGS...

THAT'S A SHAME...

THEN, AS THEY ENTER THE DREAM-ROOM...

IF YOU'RE ALL COMFORTABLE...? WE'LL BE DREAMING '**THE FIRST LANDING ON THE BLISS-WORLD OF ANSILLAR**'...YOU'LL PLAY MEMBERS OF THE SURVEY TEAM...

AH, THERE YOU ARE, K-9...BEHAVE YOUR-SELF...

AND THE NEXT THING THEY KNOW...

BY JOVE! IT'S ALMOST **REAL**...THE SPACE-SHIP... THE SUIT...

YOU DON'T NEED THE HELMET, DOCTOR ...ANSILLAR'S GOT A BREATHABLE ATMOSPHERE...

QUITE REMARKABLE! IT EVEN **SMELLS** LIKE ANOTHER WORLD!

AND LOOK AT THAT **CITY** ON THE HORIZON... SPARKLING LIKE A JEWEL!

SEVEN **MOONS**, KARITH ...THAT'S FIVE MORE THAN WE'VE GOT ON UNICEPTER...

AND THEN...

LOOK! A **PROCESSION** COMING THIS WAY...

AND THAT **MUSIC**...SO STRANGE...SO HAUNTING...

NOW THAT IS *SOME KIND* OF *WELCOMING COMMITTEE* FOR A GROUP OF OFF-WORLDERS!

BUT AS THE PROCESSION DRAWS CLOSER...

HOLD ON... THAT MAN UNDER THE CANOPY...

IT'S *LORD VEITH*! BUT...HE'S *DEAD*!

AND HE *LOOKS* IT, TOO!

THERE'S *SCYLLA* ... AND *ENOX* ... AND...

AND IF I DIDN'T KNOW BETTER I'D THINK *THEY* WERE DEAD, TOO...

LOOK!

THE FLYING NYMPHS! THEY'RE TURNING INTO...

DEVIL BIRDS!

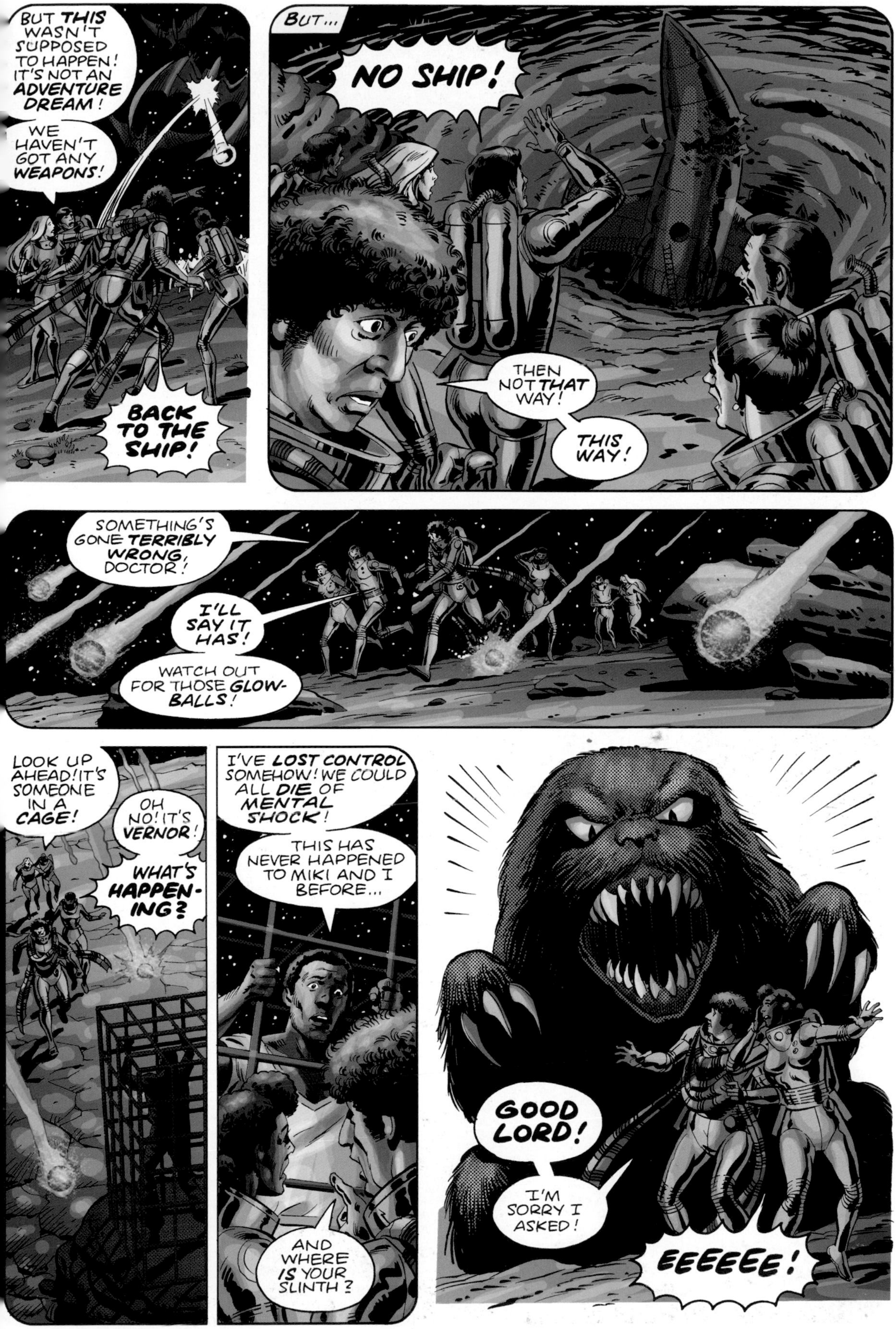
BUT THIS WASN'T SUPPOSED TO HAPPEN! IT'S NOT AN ADVENTURE DREAM!
WE HAVEN'T GOT ANY WEAPONS!
BACK TO THE SHIP!
BUT...
NO SHIP!
THEN NOT THAT WAY!
THIS WAY!
SOMETHING'S GONE TERRIBLY WRONG, DOCTOR!
I'LL SAY IT HAS!
WATCH OUT FOR THOSE GLOW-BALLS!
LOOK UP AHEAD! IT'S SOMEONE IN A CAGE!
OH NO! IT'S VERNOR!
WHAT'S HAPPEN-ING?
I'VE LOST CONTROL SOMEHOW! WE COULD ALL DIE OF MENTAL SHOCK!
THIS HAS NEVER HAPPENED TO MIKI AND I BEFORE...
AND WHERE IS YOUR SLINTH?
GOOD LORD!
I'M SORRY I ASKED!
EEEEEE!

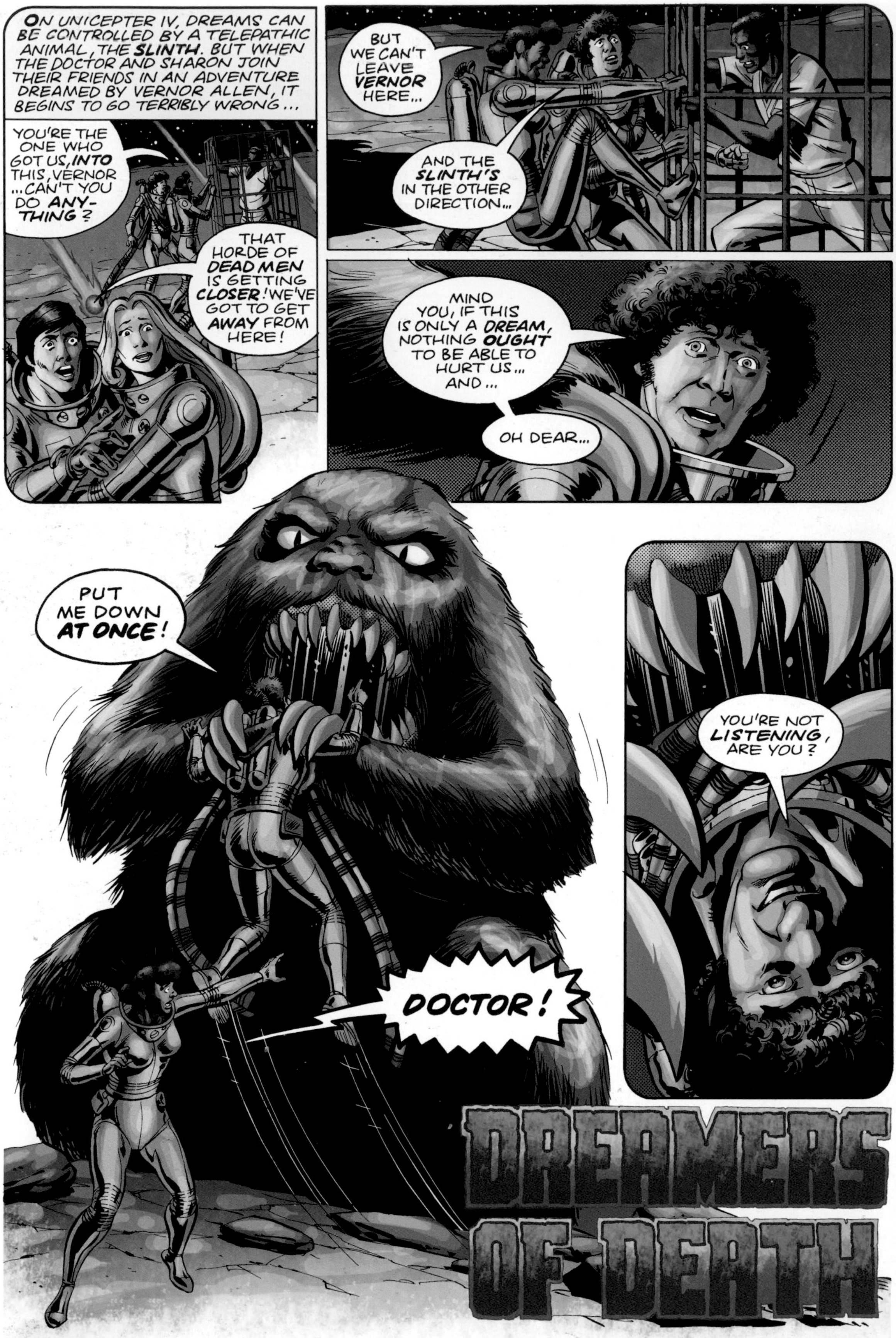

ON UNICEPTER IV, DREAMS CAN BE CONTROLLED BY A TELEPATHIC ANIMAL, THE SLINTH. BUT WHEN THE DOCTOR AND SHARON JOIN THEIR FRIENDS IN AN ADVENTURE DREAMED BY VERNOR ALLEN, IT BEGINS TO GO TERRIBLY WRONG...
YOU'RE THE ONE WHO GOT US, INTO THIS, VERNOR ...CAN'T YOU DO ANY-THING?
THAT HORDE OF DEAD MEN IS GETTING CLOSER! WE'VE GOT TO GET AWAY FROM HERE!
BUT WE CAN'T LEAVE VERNOR HERE...
AND THE SLINTH'S IN THE OTHER DIRECTION...
MIND YOU, IF THIS IS ONLY A DREAM, NOTHING OUGHT TO BE ABLE TO HURT US... AND...
OH DEAR...
PUT ME DOWN AT ONCE!
DOCTOR!
YOU'RE NOT LISTENING, ARE YOU?
DREAMERS OF DEATH

WHILE, IN THE BERRACE'S **DREAM-ROOM**, ALL SEEMS NORMAL EXCEPT...

PULSE-RATE APPROACHING CRITICAL LIMIT... BREATHING QUICKENING...

SEVERING CONNECTION, AS INSTRUCTED!

AND THE DOCTOR IS JERKED BACK TO REALITY WITH SHOCKING SUDDENNESS ...

WHAT?! I'M BACK IN THE BERRACE'S HOUSE...

THANKS, K-9...THAT WAS CLOSE...

BUT NOW I'VE GOT TO GET THE **OTHERS** OUT OF TROUBLE TOO!

AND THE EASIEST WAY IS TO CUT THINGS OFF AT THE **SOURCE**... BY TAKING VERNOR'S **DREAM-HELMET** OFF!

AND THEN...

WE'RE **BACK** ...I DIDN'T THINK WE'D **EVER** GET OUT OF THAT ...ESPECIALLY AFTER **YOU** DISAPPEARED, DOCTOR!

THOUGHT THE SLINTH HAD **KILLED** YOU...

OH, KARITH, I'VE GOT SUCH A HEAD-ACHE...

I DON'T KNOW WHAT WENT **WRONG** ...IT WAS AS IF I WAS BEING **TAKEN OVER** ... BY...

...**MIKI?**

GRRRR...

YOU'RE PROBABLY *RIGHT,* VERNOR...THIS THING'S *DANGEROUS...*

SNARRR!

IT LOOKS ALMOST... *BLOATED!*

MIKI! COME BACK!

NO, LET IT *GO!* NOW, IS EVERYONE ALRIGHT?

I THINK SO ...BUT HOW DID YOU SAVE US, DOCTOR?

I WAS *SUSPICIOUS* WHEN I HEARD ABOUT LORD VEITH BEING KILLED... AND AS THIS WAS SUPPOSED TO BE A PEACE-FUL, POETIC DREAM ...

I TOLD *K-9* TO MONITOR MY REACTIONS... SO IF I GOT TOO *EXCITED,* HE'D *BREAK* THE CONNECTION...

BUT I STILL DON'T UNDERSTAND ...WE'VE NEVER HAD TROUBLE WITH SLINTHS *BEFORE...*

HOLD ON ...THAT'S THE *GENERAL ALARM SIREN* ...I'D BETTER SWITCH ON THE *VIS-NEWS!*

VWEE!! VWEE!!

REPORTS ARE COMING IN OF A NUMBER OF *FATAL ACCIDENTS* INVOLVING DREAMERS AND THEIR CLIENTS ...

THE *SLINTHS* ARE BELIEVED TO BE RESPONSIBLE, AND IT IS FEARED THAT THE DEATH-TOLL MAY RUN INTO *HUNDREDS* ...

YOU ARE THEREFORE ADVISED *NOT TO DREAM* UNDER ANY CIRCUMSTANCES...

SLINTHS ARE TO BE REGARDED AS *VERMIN* AND *DESTROYED!*

THIS IS **TERRIBLE**! SLINTHS ARE **GOOD** ...THEY GIVE US DREAMS...

BUT **YOU** HAVEN'T BEEN GIVING THEM ANYTHING IN **RETURN** ...AND NOTHING'S **FREE**!

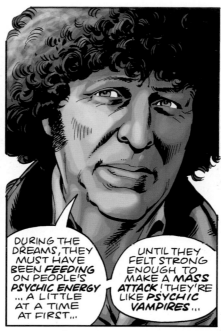

DURING THE DREAMS, THEY MUST HAVE BEEN **FEEDING** ON PEOPLE'S **PSYCHIC ENERGY** ...A LITTLE AT A TIME AT FIRST...

UNTIL THEY FELT STRONG ENOUGH TO MAKE A **MASS ATTACK**! THEY'RE LIKE **PSYCHIC VAMPIRES**...

YOU'RE PROBABLY **RIGHT**...

BUT LIFE'S GOING TO SEEM AWFULLY **EMPTY** WITHOUT THAT FRIENDLY LITTLE FURBALL SITTING ON MY SHOULDER ...SHARING MY THOUGHTS...

BUT THEN...

RESIDENTS IN THE **4TH** AND **5TH** DISTRICTS ARE URGED TO **EVACUATE** THEIR HOMES...

A HUGE **UNIDENTIFIED CREATURE** HAS BEEN SPOTTED STALKING THE STREETS...

THAT'S THE OTHER SIDE OF THE RIVER...

COME ON SHARON, K-9 ...I'VE GOT A **NASTY FEELING** ABOUT THIS...

YOU'D **BETTER** KEEP YOUR FAMILY HERE, GARRET, WHERE THEY'RE **SAFE**...

WAIT! I'LL COME WITH YOU...!

AND SOON...

BLIMEY! LOOK AT **THAT**!

IT'S A HUGE **DEVIL**... LIKE THEY USED TO BELIEVE IN ON **EARTH**!

BECAUSE *FEAR* AND *TERROR* GENERATE MOST *PSYCHIC ENERGY* FOR THEM TO *FEED ON...*

HERE COMES THE *MILITARY...*

AND WHILE THE SLINTHS WERE IN TELEPATHIC COMMUNION WITH YOU *DREAMERS*, THEY REACHED BACK INTO YOUR MINDS FOR THE MOST TERRIBLE IMAGE THEY COULD FIND... *THE DEVIL!*

OKAY, MEN! *BLAST IT WITH EVERYTHING YOU'VE GOT!*

BUT ITS BODY'S MADE UP OF *HUNDREDS OF SLINTHS...* ACTING TOGETHER AS A *GROUP MIND* ...WITH A *SINGLE BODY*

BUT WHY MAKE A *DEVIL?*

BUT...

IT'S NOT *WORKING!* WE'RE HITTING IT WITH *THORSEN-303'S...* AND IT'S JUST *SOAKING THEM UP!*

IN FACT...IT'S GETTING *BIGGER!*

TELL YOUR MEN TO *CEASE FIRE*, CAPTAIN! THE SLINTHS ARE JUST *ABSORBING THE ENERGY!*

OLD-FASHIONED *PROJECTILE WEAPONS* MIGHT WORK, BUT...

COME ON, SHARON... WE'LL BE BACK, DOCTOR...

AT LEAST IT SEEMS TO BE STAYING ON *THAT SIDE* OF THE RIVER...

PERHAPS SLINTHS DON'T LIKE WATER...

IN THE BRIEF LULL THAT FOLLOWS...

WE'VE GOT ALL THE EMERGENCY SERVICES HERE...FIRE, AMBULANCE, POLICE...

BUT IF THAT THING CROSSES OVER...

CAPTAIN! IT'S MOVING TOWARDS THOSE POWER-LINES!

IT'S ABSORBING ENERGY FROM THE CABLES! EATING ELECTRICITY!

QUICK! DESTROY THAT PYLON!

AND, AS THORSEN-303'S MELT STRUTS...

SPFAAZZ!

ZZAAF!

THE CABLE'S DOWN...BUT IT'S GOT SO MUCH BIGGER!

MAYBE BIG ENOUGH TO STEP EASILY OVER THE RIVER...

MAYBE I CAN SLOW IT DOWN! SHARON AND I...UH ...STOLE THIS OLD BULLET-FIRING RIFLE FROM THE MUSEUM...

COURSE, I HATE TO THINK ONE OF THE SLINTHS I SHOOT MIGHT BE MIKI, BUT...

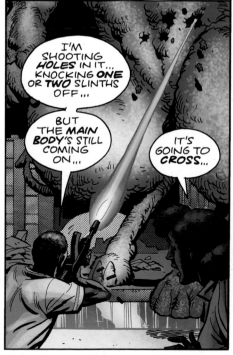

I'M SHOOTING HOLES IN IT... KNOCKING ONE OR TWO SLINTHS OFF...

BUT THE MAIN BODY'S STILL COMING ON...

IT'S GOING TO CROSS...

LOOK OUT! SHARON! IT'S TRYING TO CRUSH US!

YIII!

QUICK! GET ME TWENTY YARDS OF *BARE CABLE!*

NOW, COME HERE, *K-9!* I'VE GOT A *JOB* FOR YOU!

IT'S *ACROSS!* THERE'S NO WAY WE CAN *STOP* IT! WE'LL HAVE TO *WITH-DRAW!*

PULL OUT! EVERYONE *EVACUATE!*

AHA! OF COURSE... *THAT'S* WHY THE SLINTHS AVOIDED THE RIVER!

AND, INSTANTS LATER...

ALRIGHT, K-9 ...I WANT YOU TO TAKE THIS CABLE ...AND HEAD TOWARDS THAT BRUTE...

THEN LOOP IT ROUND THE THING'S ANKLE...

BUT JUST AS K-9 COMPLETES HIS TASK...

HE'S *STOPPED*, DOCTOR... WHAT'S GONE *WRONG*?

NO TIME FOR THAT NOW, SHARON...

WHERE'S THAT FIRE-ENGINE?

B-BUT... DOCTOR?...

THAT THING'S BLOATED WITH *ELECTRICAL ENERGY*...

SO IF I *DOUSE* IT WITH *WATER*,..

ZZZAKK!

ZZAPP!

SPFAZZ!

IT'S *SHORTING OUT!* THE CABLE'S DRAINING IT!

AND IT'S *SHRINKING!*

NOW IT'S *FALLING APART* ...THE SLINTHS ARE RETURNING TO *NORMAL SIZE*...

WE'LL SOON *MOP THEM UP* NOW!

THANKS, DOCTOR-- WHOEVER YOU ARE...

HOW'S *K-9?*

HE'LL BE ALRIGHT! THAT THING DRAINED *HIS* ELECTRICITY, TOO... BUT IT'S JUST A *FLAT BATTERY!*

AND SO, A COUPLE OF DAYS LATER, AT THE BERRACE'S HOUSE...

IT'S BEEN GOOD TO SEE YOU AGAIN, GARRET... BUT I'D BETTER TRY TO GET *SHARON HOME* AGAIN...

ER, DOCTOR ...I THINK *THIS* IS GOING TO BE HOME FROM NOW ON...

THERE'S NOTHING FOR ME TO GO BACK TO *BLACKCASTLE* FOR... NOT SINCE I *GREW UP* ...

AND *VERNOR'S* GOING TO HAVE TO MAKE A *NEW LIFE* FOR HIM- SELF NOW THERE'S NO MORE DREAMING ...SO WE THOUGHT WE'D *START TOGETHER...*

WE'LL LOOK AFTER HER, DOCTOR, DON'T WORRY...

WELL, I'LL MISS YOU, SHARON...

BUT K-9 AND I HAD BETTER GO...

COME BACK AND SEE US SOMETIME, DOCTOR!

I'LL *TRY,* SHARON ...BUT YOU KNOW THE *TARDIS*...

IF I SET THE CONTROLS FOR *UNICEPTER* ...IT'LL PROBABLY PUT ME IN *BLACK- CASTLE!*

THE END.

Artwork by Joe Corroney

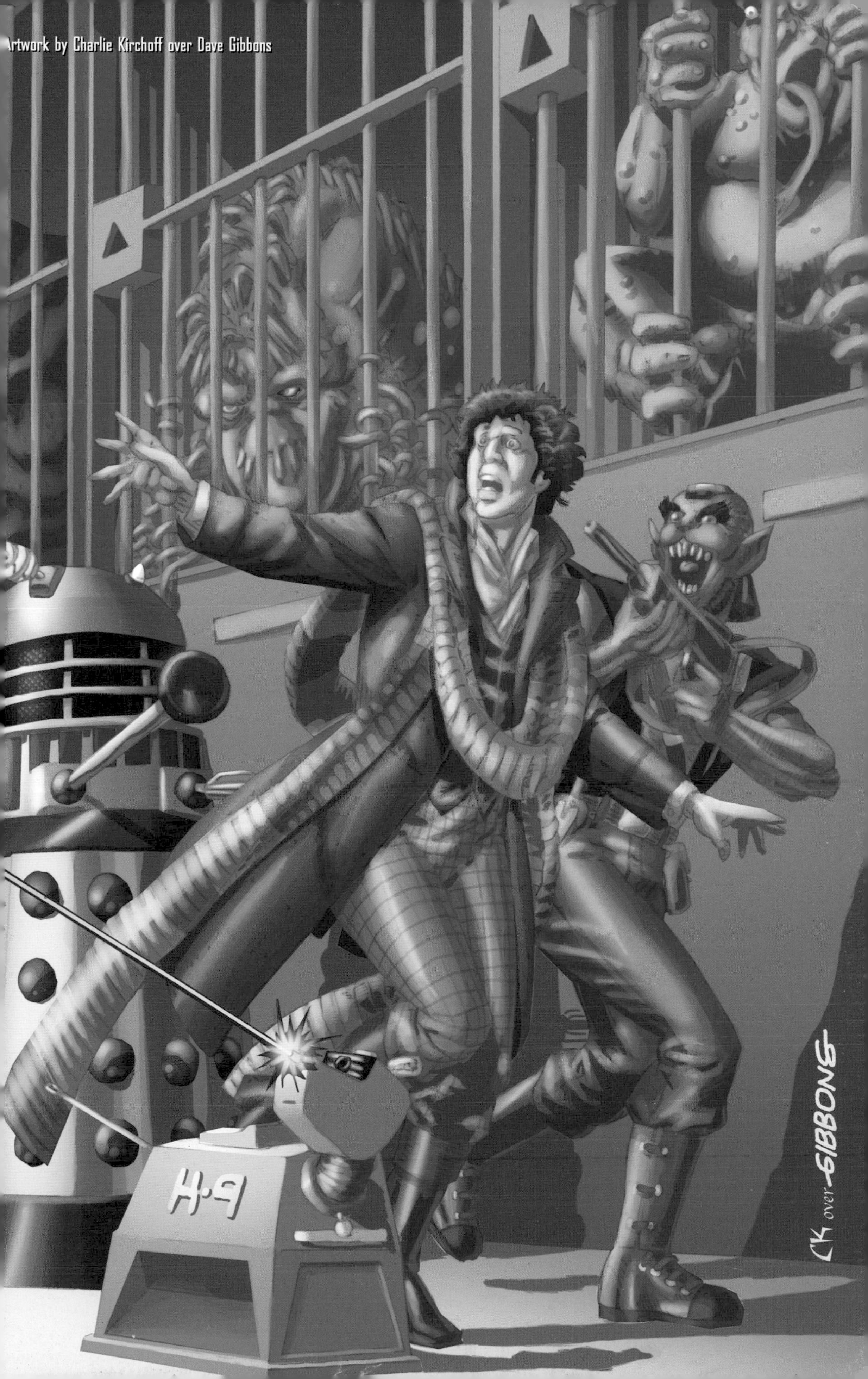
CK over GIBBONS

Artwork by Charlie Kirchoff over Dave Gibbons

Artwork by Charlie Kirchoff over Dave Gibbons

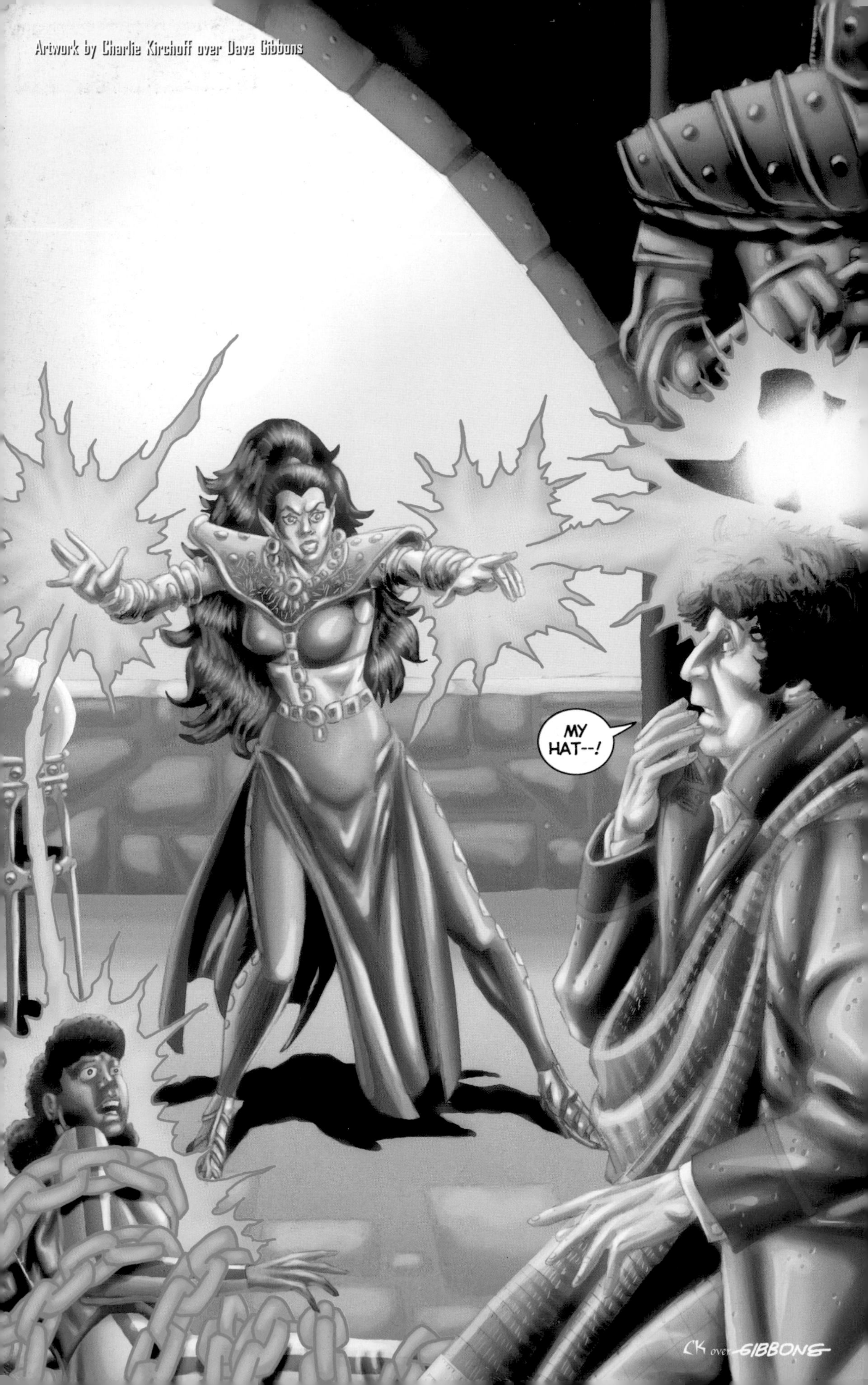
MY HAT--!
CK over GIBBONS

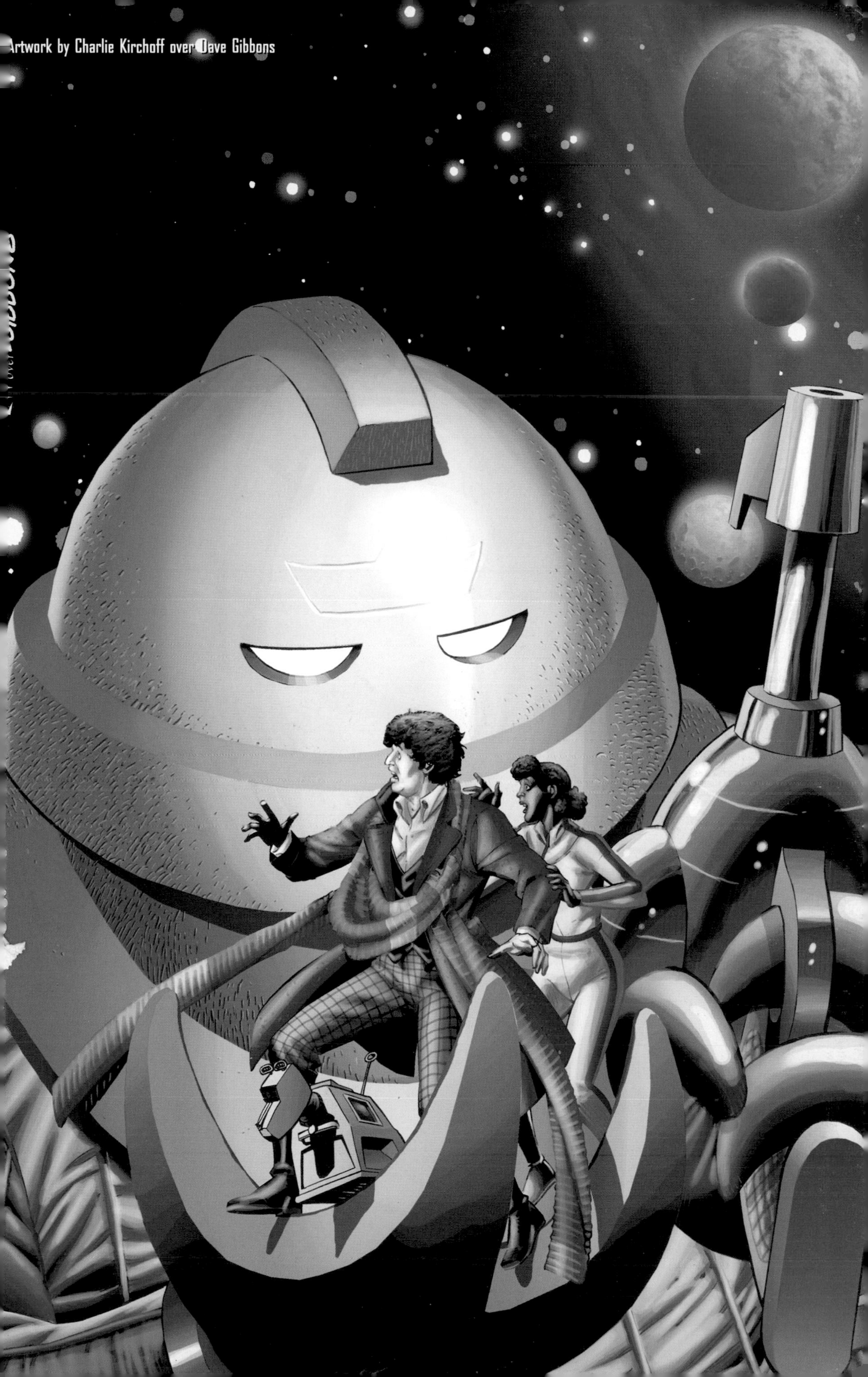

Artwork by Charlie Kirchoff over Dave Gibbons

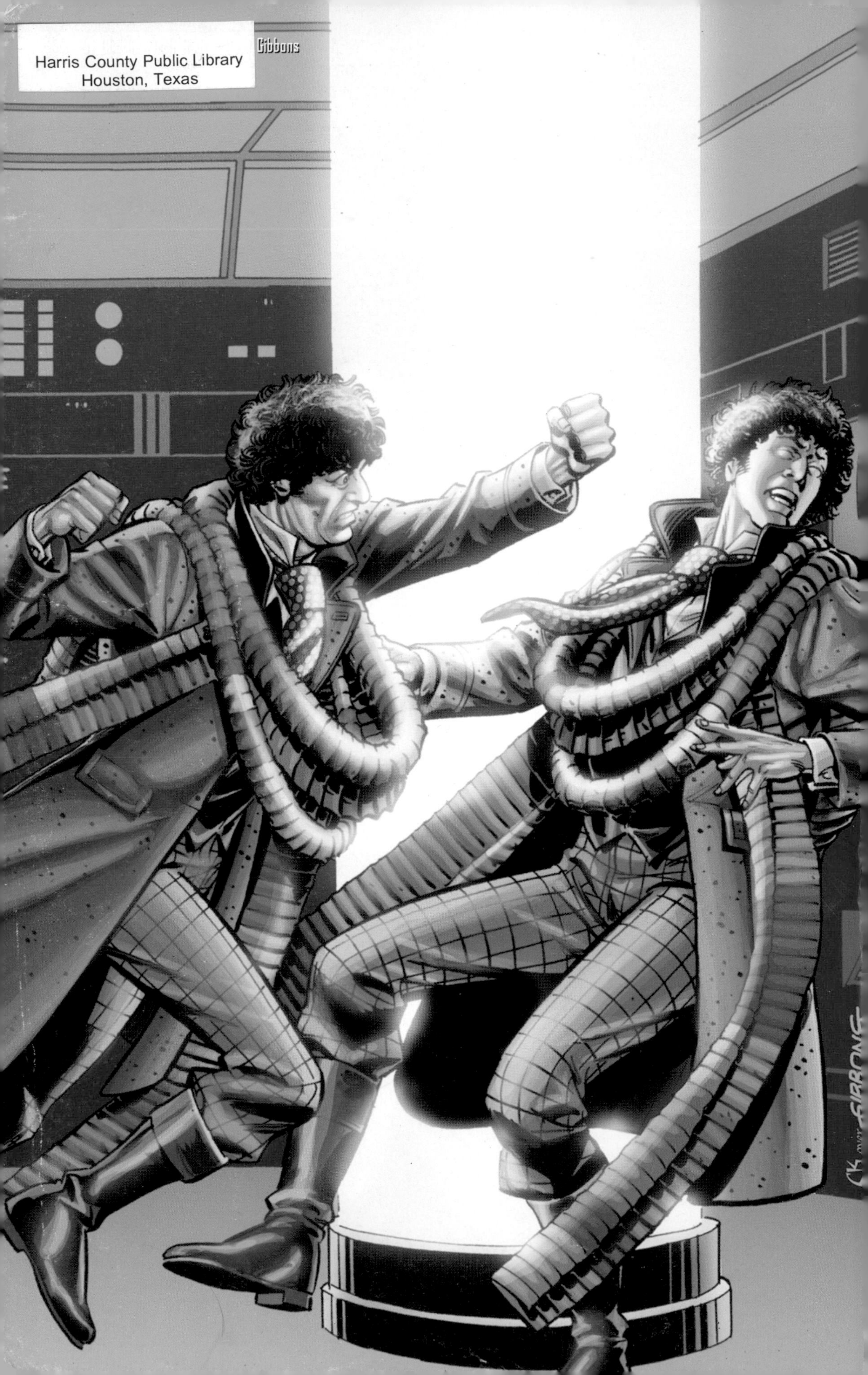
Gibbons